The
55 Laws
Of Real Estate
Investing

A Road Map To
Real Estate Success

By

Jeff Leighton

Important Disclaimers

Table of Contents

Author's Note

This book contains additional resources that I use on a daily basis as a real estate investor. Since I could not physically include these in the book, they are all available to download for free on my website www.jeff-leighton.com. That includes my deal analyzer, repair estimator, example contracts, marketing pieces that I use, recommended resources, helpful videos, and much more.

Introduction

The 55 Laws of Real Estate Investing is a guidebook on the art of real estate investing. The laws in this book are based on successful multimillionaire and real estate investors who have mastered their craft, in addition to my own experiences as a full-time real estate investor. These laws are an accumulation of only the best wisdom and ideas from the top real estate investors in the country and in history.

The premise behind these laws is simple: observe these laws if you want to make more money in real estate investing and be more successful as a real estate investor. I have written this guide with numerous stories from my own experiences and practical examples and lessons learned along the way with each law of real estate investing.

This book is not meant to be a textbook; instead, it is a straight-to-the-point action guide that should be read or referenced several times to internalize these timeless principles. While I cannot guarantee that you will make a million dollars tomorrow from reading this guide, I *can* ensure that you will become a savvier and better real estate investor, no matter what your experience level is. You may be familiar with some of these concepts, but chances are, most of them will be unique insights and ideas. So let's jump into it.

The Force Multiplier Effect

When looking for real estate deals, you should never rely on just one source of leads. This is not only dangerous, but it's also ineffective. You need to build a strong foundation with the way you source your deals or your marketing. Jay Abraham, a legendary marketer, has a principle known as the "force multiplier effect," which can be applied to real estate investing as well as many other businesses out there.

It relates to a military-style attack of creating multiple ways of penetrating the enemy or, in this case, penetrating the market by coming in through an air attack, sea attack, stealth attack, and land attack. This is a proven military process that relates to real estate investing when it comes to your marketing.

The savvy real estate investors out there who consistently find the best deals have multiple avenues of finding deals. Instead of just relying on one local real estate agent or doing a few pieces of direct mail, the top investors might be sending out thousands of direct mail pieces a month, have an entire team of real estate agents looking for deals, have a comprehensive SEO and pay per click online marketing campaign, network extensively with other investors, as well as use other sources of lead generation.

When you are taking that much action and coming from that many angles, you will find that there are plenty of good deals out there. The investors who can't find deals are often the ones that only have one strategy and put forward just a minimal effort towards it.

Overall, keep in mind that when you are getting started as a real estate investor, you should start with just one lead source and master that before trying to move on to the next one. However, once you get your first source of leads down, let's say it's direct mail or online marketing, you should then try to expand to the next one and the next one and, ideally, have at least three sources of solid lead generation streams coming in.

The idea is to have so many leads coming in from so many different angles that you can cherry-pick the best ones. No matter how competitive your market is or how competitive you think it is, you will find deals when you use this strategy.

LAW #2

Multiple Streams Of Income

If you want to become successful and build a real estate empire, you need to develop multiple streams of income within the real estate investing industry. All of the top investors do it. If you start now, you can build massive streams of income in different parts of the business. Since many of these are complementary skills, there is no reason not to have at least three or four streams of income.

These could include rehabbing, wholesaling, being a licensed agent, buying rental properties, doing private money lending on deals or investing in crowdfunding, and joint venturing with newer investors.

To protect yourself against the economy and to build a strong business foundation, you should have multiple streams of income. It is too dangerous nowadays and not proactive to rely on just rehabs or wholesales as your sole source of income. While you should have a focus as to what your main exit strategy is, you should also look into adding complimentary streams of income to your business.

As one example, I know a local couple that does a lot of investing and also has their real estate license. In between the flips they are doing, they also make money from being an agent since they have a good eye for investments and a lot of experience.

If you don't want to be an agent, but you are getting a lot of leads, you could always refer leads to a local agent you know and trust. Most of the leads you get will not fit the investor model, but they would be perfect for an agent.

Some investors might also be building a portfolio

of rental properties to give them income between their flips. With each successful flip they will put a portion of that income towards increasing their passive income with rentals. As a house flipper, you will come across good flip opportunities as well as good rental property opportunities so you always need to be ready.

Another source of income for more experienced investors is lending money to other experienced investors. If you have done a lot of deals and understand how to evaluate a rehab deal, you can often get 10-12 percent on your money on a short-term basis with a private money loan.

Or if you don't have the necessary capital to invest in a big rehab, you can always invest in real estate crowdfunding, which is another source of passive income. All you need is about $500 to get started and you can start investing on places like Fundrise and others.

Lastly, if you have a successful track record of investing, you could often partner with local up-and-coming real estate investors to teach them the ropes of the business. I have many investor friends who mentor newer real estate investors in their area for free. Once the newer investor finds a deal, the experienced investor will partner with them 50/50. There are countless ways to start building additional streams of income.

Overall, as you gain more experience as a real estate investor, you should focus on building your income streams. Maybe one arm of your business focuses on wholesaling, one is rehabbing, in another you do real estate agent deals or refer them to agents, in a fourth you lend money on discounted real estate deals, and then in a fifth, you partner with newer investors.

Ideally, you should have at least three sources of income. Warren Buffett said, "Never rely on a single source of income." The great thing about real estate is that there are plenty of practical ways to create additional revenue sources. Don't be the one-trick pony who is still only fixing up houses 20 years into the business. It is much riskier and much harder to scale your business if you only focus on one source of income.

The Offer Formula

Any time you buy a house as an investment, whether it's a short-term flip or longer-term hold, you need to have a formula for buying houses. You must have a systematized way of evaluating deals that considers all the costs when it comes to investing.

There are often many more costs associated with investing than you are aware of and by having a deal analyzer is a simple solution to that. It will tell you exactly how much you are predicted to make or lose. You need to have an idea of what the potential profit of any deal is before going into it.

If you are getting started as a real estate investor,

it can be tempting to think that any property that is listed below market value is automatically a deal. I see many investors think that if you buy a house at 200K, put 50K into it, and then sell it at 300K, then you have made a 50K profit.

They are of course not considering closing costs, real estate agent fees, taxes, insurance, and other fees that can eat into a profit. I thought along the same lines when I was getting started: if it was just a good amount lower than the sales price, then there must be a profit in there somewhere. This is completely wrong and will get you in trouble.

I see articles all the time in the media that say the average investor makes 40K or 50K on a property because they bought a house at 250K and sold it at 300K. The problem is, the majority of these articles leave out a little something us investors like to call expenses. In many cases, I can guarantee you the investor was probably losing money on these deals since the media does not account for expenses, but focuses on what they bought it for and what they sold it for.

While the average re-sale might be 50K or 60k

higher, the average profit is certainly not 50K or 60K. Only the experienced investors are making those kinds of profits. Do not fall into the trap of this misrepresentation by mainstream media. In order to make 50K per deal, you must use a deal analyzer.

Overall, you need to know the exact profit potential of any deal so that you don't make a big mistake. There are two ways of doing this. The first is to use what's called the MAO or Maximum Allowable Offer formula. This means that the most you can pay for a deal is the ARV or after renovated value times .7 minus the cost of repairs.

So if a property will sell for 300K in renovated condition, you would multiply this times .7. That would give you 210K and then you would subtract 50K for repairs if that's the repair number, which would leave you with 160K as the most you could pay for the property. When getting started, you must use this formula.

A second and more specific way of using an offer formula is to have a deal analyzer. Your deal analyzer should tell you the exact amount you are making as well as the exact percent of profit you are making. Also, if you are a newer investor, I would not touch any deal under 10% profit. You should be around 15%.

It is more common for newer investors to underestimate repair costs or overvalue the after renovated value. You need to be very conservative to do well in real estate investing and every real estate investor needs a deal analyzer. If you want to download the one I use, go to my website, www.jeff-leighton.com, to get a copy today.

Grand Slams

The goal with real estate investing is similar to playing baseball: you need to get on base. If you focus on getting on base and doing consistent deals, the home runs and grand slams will come. However, you should not try to swing for the grand slams every time, especially if it's your very first couple of deals.

I recently met with a newer investor who was asking me about developing 10 townhomes in a neighborhood when he had never even done one flip before. This was a disaster waiting to happen, and I told him so.

I always recommend working your way up to the bigger deals. Too many investors try to make

100K or 200K on their very first deal. Instead you should try to wholesale a few deals to more experienced investors, do a couple of light rehab projects, or buy a local rental property or two. When you are getting started as an investor, there is a lot more risk, so you need to be more conservative.

If you are consistently marketing in this business, you will come across the solid six-figure deals a couple of times per year, but you should not be trying to force those deals. What I mean by that is, if you need to do a massive two-story addition and are using comps from a different neighborhood to justify making a huge profit on a deal, then it's probably not a deal. The best investors are steady and consistent and look for profitable deals where they can make at least 15%.

Overall, if you are a newer investor, you should start on smaller projects or wholesale deals and then work your way up. Focus on doing a successful real estate investment deal first and foremost, and don't try to squeeze out every last dollar when you are getting started. If you decide to venture off and do something like building a million-dollar spec home or developing a townhouse community for the first time, you need to be extremely careful.

I've seen even super savvy experienced investors get burned by trying to hit a grand slam with some type of development deal that they didn't have too much experience with. One company I know bought land for hundreds of thousands of dollars only to find out they were not allowed to build houses there.

Another investor tried to develop a luxury community when his background was as a real estate agent and things didn't work out too well. On the flip side of things, one of the largest and most successful real estate developers in my city got his start by flipping small row homes before moving his way up to billion-dollar developments.

I'm not against trying new things, but I think it should be incremental. Learn how to wholesale, or do smaller scale renovations before you take on massive projects like condo conversions or new development that could yield a ton of profit but also come with a lot of risks.

Rule Of 100

Since real estate investing is such a significant investment with the potential to make a big profit, you need to be very selective about which deal you buy. Many real estate investors, including real estate mogul Grant Cardone, talk about the rule of 100, where you should look at and evaluate at least 100 different deals before buying one.

This does not necessarily mean you have to see each property in person, but you should properly take 100 deals through your analysis before pulling the trigger. This will make you much more successful than if you just looked at the first ten deals you saw and decided to buy one.

If you are getting started with real estate investing, this is especially true. I see it happen way too often that just because a property is listed for sale or looks dilapidated in their neighborhood, a newer investor thinks it's a great deal. While it certainly could be a good deal, you need to look at a minimum of 100 deals – especially if you are a newer investor.

After looking at 100, you will realize that most properties out there are not good deals and you will get a much clearer understanding of the business, different neighborhoods in your area, and what to look for with deals. For example, in my business now, I look at 50-100 off-market leads before buying one property. And you can bet that the property I do buy is a cream of the crop deal because I have qualified through so many leads.

Overall, you need to understand a couple of things. When you are getting started, it can be dangerous to jump on the first deal you see because you are so excited about the business. Instead, make sure you put at least 100 deals through your deal analyzer. That will help you learn what price points you need to be buying at depending on the neighborhood and type of property.

Next, you should have a solid marketing foundation that is bringing in tons of leads every month. This will allow you to focus on only the best deals in the market. Typically, the way it works is that I might get 100 leads, have only about 20 good leads, and have about five amazing leads, which will be the properties I try to get under contract. If you only get ten leads a month and you have to buy one of them, it might not be the best deal.

Nothing Cheap

Real estate investors can sometimes be seen as people that cut corners and take the easy or cheap road. You need to be sure as an investor that you not only not take the cheap or easy way out, but you don't even want to give the impression that any corners were cut. The minute a potential buyer of your deals thinks that you are an amateur cutting corners, it can pollute the whole deal, and they will view any and all of your work as being low-quality.

There are a couple of specific things that real estate investors tend to do when selling their deal which can come across as cheap or low-quality. This lesson is just in regard to selling your property. When doing the work, make sure you use a licensed, recommended contractor and that they pull any necessary permits. When selling your property, it needs to be properly optimized for the market.

That means a couple of things. For starters, you should not try to do a for sale by owner or try to list the property yourself unless you are already an established agent. Nothing comes across as cheaper and jankier than a for sale by owner listing. Many times, these properties are not taken seriously and have a stigma of being unrealistic sellers with unrealistic prices.

I recommend finding a local real estate agent with an excellent reputation and a track record of selling properties quickly and for the right price. Many times, investors try to list their properties at significantly higher prices than the market is selling at and they will sit and sit without any buyers. That is why you need a local agent who can list it at the right price and handle the negotiations for you.

The second thing you must do when selling a property is getting a professional photographer. I can't tell you how many times investors take photos themselves on their iPhones. Since just about everybody looks at photos online before seeing a property in person, bad pictures can immediately eliminate someone's interest in a house. Make sure your agent gets professional photography done. Usually, it's only several hundred dollars, and any good agent will include that in their listing service.

Lastly, make sure your property is staged by a professional. I know it sounds kind of gimmicky, but having been in real estate investing for almost ten years now, we stage every single property because they sell faster. Many buyers of homes cannot picture the furniture or layout when they see a property without staging. When nobody lives there, a property can seem cold and uninviting.

The key to this concept as a real estate investor is not to cut corners and make sure you do these three items when selling any property. If you look at ten houses on the MLS on any given day, I can guarantee you that most of them do not have professional photography, are not staged, or might be listed by the owner themselves at a discount.

If you properly optimize your property with a good local agent, professional photos, and staging, it will be in the top percent of houses on the market. At the very least, you will get a ton of traffic through the door.

—◆—◆—◆—

Everyone Is Your Partner

You should see everyone as a potential partner, including your direct competition. This will open up the doors of possibility in the real estate investing world. Too many people think that real estate investing is oversaturated, too competitive, and there are no more deals out there.

The only problem with this is that you can go back and see that people have been saying that for the last several decades, yet there have been successful new investors every single year and there will continue to be.

I was just reading a book written in the '80s that said the real estate investing business is now too competitive. Every industry and every business already has enough of whatever service or product they are offering; however, it's up to you to create your own market and niche.

There is a fortune to be made when you start considering your competition as partners, and it will open up a new gateway of deals and opportunities.

When I was getting started in real estate investing, after I did three deals, I thought there would probably not be many more deals out there because I had just taken off a lot of the inventory. In reality, there are thousands and thousands of potential deals out there. You will soon realize this after being in the business for a while. Not only that, but there will be an endless number of deals out there once you start to see your so-called competition as your partner.

I can't tell you how many times one of my competitors has referred me a deal they were too busy to work on or how many times they have offered to lend private money on one of my deals instead of paying higher hard money rates. Sometimes I even partner with a wholesaler friend of mine who has 10,000 people on his buyer list.

Even though we are going after the same deals, if I get a property under contract and since I don't have that big of a buyer list, I can send my deal out on his list, and we both get paid and are happy. Since he has so many people on his list, I just have to find properties that are a little bit under MLS values. Chances are, there's a buyer for that deal. It's opened up a whole new stream of deals.

Another way you could partner with your competition is to see if they would be willing to lend private money on your deals or even become your competition's top lender if you have funds available. Some investors have too many leads and not enough money, while other investors have too much money and not enough leads. By networking and building relationships with other real estate investing pros, you will find additional ways to do deals.

A third way of investors doing deals with their competition is by partnering with new investors. If you are a seasoned investor, you can take an up-and-coming investor under your wings and help them get their first couple of deals under contract in exchange for 50 percent of the deal.

Likewise, if you are the newer investors, for your first couple of deals you work out partnerships with the top investors who will help you get your deal to closing in exchange for a piece of the deal. There are a million ways to create more deal opportunities that most people overlook because they don't want anything to do with their competition.

Overall, have an abundance mentality and look for ways to partner with the competition when it makes sense. Just by doing this, you will create a whole new avenue of deals. The top investors in any market will do co-wholesaling with their competition, work out lending arrangements with their competition, and might even train new investors on how to bring them deals.

There are countless other ways to partner with your competition limited only by your own creativity. Keep an open mind and try to build as many connections with your competition as possible. You might even learn some of their best strategies along the way.

Get A Mentor

I'm not sure which real estate investor said this, but he was saying, "It's crazy how, if you want to become a dentist, you go to dental school, a doctor goes to medical school, but so many real estate investors just wing it and don't get educated at all." I'm not saying the training for learning real estate investing is as intense as medical school, but you must get specialized education as a real estate investor because you will pay one way or another.

You will pay either with a mentor or for the mistakes you make, and it's better to invest in the mentor – trust me. Real estate investing is a journey filled with ups, downs, and everything in between. If you want to be successful in your journey, you must align yourself with a mentor.

There are several different ways of going about finding a mentor, and you must choose at least one. The stakes in this business are too high not to have someone in your corner that can show you the ropes and take you to the next level.

Nearly every successful real estate investor or business person started as a protégé to someone and had a mentor that they followed. Now, there are several ways of getting mentors, and you should rely on ALL of them if you want to be successful. I've had numerous mentors. Try to find the best ideas from each of them, since every successful real estate investor has a slightly different interpretation of the business.

One of the first ways of getting a mentor is by listening to or reading different interviews of real estate investors. Fortunately, there are countless free podcasts and free information out there where you can hear about how different investors got started, their challenges, where they are now, and what advice they would give to newer investors in terms of finding and closing deals.

This should give you a good framework for the business. These interviews should point you in the right direction regarding marketing ideas, next steps, and what type of investing you should be doing.

Another way of getting a mentor is by finding who the top local investors in your area are and starting to send them any leads you dig up. The best way to find out who the top local investors are is simple. Just go to REIA (real estate investor association) meetings, Meetup groups, and search online for the "we buy houses" companies. You will start to see the same names over and over again – chances are, those are the top investors.

Then start reaching out to them and ask them what types of deals they are looking for. Many times, they like to partner with new local investors who bring them leads. They will help you put the deals together, and all you have to do is bring them qualified, vetted, off-market leads. After a few deals with them, you will see how the top investors operate. It's a great learning experience.

Lastly, there are numerous real estate mentor programs where you pay for a successful real estate investor to mentor you. That is what I did when I first got started in the business in addition to using the other two strategies mentioned here.

What I like about mentorship programs is that, when you pay a good amount of money for something, you tend to value it a lot more than just a free YouTube video. As a result of paying for the program, I put my heart and soul into making real estate investing work one way or another. Fortunately, I had an excellent education and mentorship program that I am still involved with today.

Overall, you must have a mentor as a real estate investor, and I would recommend having several mentors. Each mentor might have a different angle on the real estate investing industry, and there is something to be learned from any successful real estate investor, no matter what part of the country they are in and what type of real estate investing they do.

You should use all three of the aforementioned mentorship strategies if you want to have the most advantages going for you. Do not be the person that tries to do everything on their own without any help. That is who Russel Brunson refers to as the "pioneers." You can tell if someone is a pioneer because they have all the arrows in their back. If you follow a proven path from a successful investor, you will be much more successful.

LAW #9

───◆───────◆───

Market Appreciation

When buying a flip, you should never purchase it for potential appreciation. Flips are short-term, meaning that you are in and out within three to six months. During that time, the market could go up or it could go down, but you should never depend on that to make your numbers work.

The investors that went belly up during the market crash were the amateurs who were speculatively buying houses like that with no strategy outside of hoping the market would appreciate. The difference between the big boys of real estate and those that were exposed as amateurs just riding the wave of appreciation was that the former use the MAO (maximum allowable offer) formula for buying properties and sort through many leads to find the best ones.

I believe in buying properties for potential future appreciation – just not flips. If you plan to hold on to a property for five or 10 years in a developing area, then that's fine. It's a little bit speculative, but as long as a lot is going on in the area, that's great. What you should avoid at all costs, though, is buying a short-term flip for potential appreciation.

That gets you into a very dangerous territory that can quickly see your flip turn upside down. Things can happen that are entirely out of your control, and it is a gamble if you decide to predict what the economy will do. I have not met anyone yet that can predict the economy and the real estate market, despite the fact that many real estate agents and investors claim to know.

The most dangerous thing I have ever heard is, "I'm only losing X amount per year," in reference to buying near big potential development areas. I've seen it happen many times: people buy on pure speculation, but developments can become stalled – if they even get started –, the economy could crash, or any number of things out of your control could happen. That is exactly what amateur flippers during the 2007 crash said before they lost everything.

Overall, remember that you don't control the economy and, despite what you think, you cannot predict the economy. That means you have to buy houses for short-term flips with the MAO formula, because you *can* control that. That formula is what kept the professional house flippers in business during downturns in the economy and weeded out the amateur professionals who were buying on pure speculation.

It's okay if you buy a house to live in or rent out with the idea that it might appreciate several years down the road, but stay as far away as possible from the short-term appreciation expectations with flipping. In a booming economic time, it can be very easy to fall into that trap.

LAW #10

Off-Market Deals

The best real estate investing deals are the ones that never hit the MLS. When a property is listed, it is often seen by thousands and thousands of agents and investors driving the price up and entering bidding wars.

While you can find great deals on the MLS, if you are strategic about it, it is far better to purchase your property directly from a motivated seller who is not looking to list the property. The top investors all try to buy their houses off the market. With just some basic marketing skills, you too should be able to purchase off-market properties consistently.

When I say "off-market," I mean not listed on the

market with a real estate agent. I'm not referring to FSBOs, which some agents try to portray as off-market to boost their credentials. Those are technically speaking off-market deals, but they also have some of the most non-motivated sellers on the planet, usually at unrealistically high prices. Off-market deals can be generated in several different ways, but there are three ways in particular that I recommend for finding them.

The first one is direct mail to an already pre-qualified group of sellers that are motivated, including absentee-owned properties, vacant/blighted houses, pre-foreclosure, probate, tax lien, and any other potentially motivated seller.

Keep in mind that your response rate with direct mail will typically only be around 1%. However, all you also don't need 100 leads or anything; 25 leads should get you right in the ballpark of getting an amazing off-market deal with a lot of potential.

The second way of getting an off-market deal is doing online marketing, including SEO or search engine optimization around the keywords "sell house fast," "we buy houses," and other similarly motivated keywords that a seller might be typing in. You should optimize for those keywords on your website, blog, YouTube videos, and any other type of online marketing you do.

To make your online marketing even more effective, you can add a pay per click campaign around those motivated keywords. The best part about PPC or pay per click is that you are only charged when someone clicks on your ad, and you can start with any amount, no matter how small or large your budget is. Just make sure you set a limit because you will get people clicking on the ad and could spend a lot of money quickly.

Lastly, if you are looking for a fantastic off-market deal, you should try to find the 20-25 wholesalers in your area and get on their email list for off-market deals. A good wholesaler will send you off-market properties that are discounted. If you have at least 20, then you will see a lot of potential opportunities, and you can cherry-pick the best one.

The fastest ways to build a big list of wholesalers is by networking at REIAs, doing research on

LinkedIn for wholesalers in your area, and writing down any bandit sign you see that says "we buy houses cash" and a phone number. Those strategies should easily give you at least 20 wholesalers that can start emailing you weekly off-market deals, in addition to your direct mail and the online marketing you do.

Overall, with off-market deals, the way to be successful is to be strategic with how you find deals. Most investors have no strategy whatsoever or make so little effort that they have no chance of finding deals.

That means, if you decide to do direct mail, you should only send mail to motivated sellers, and you need to send at least three letters over the course of six months. Most investors never do that; they make a minimal effort by sending 50 letters out the door one time, and then they say direct mail doesn't work.

Or with your online marketing, you should make a list of the most motivated keywords a seller might be typing in and then target all your online ads around those keywords. Then get set up with a solid PPC campaign so that you have the online marketing covered on both the paid and organic search angles.

Lastly, try to recruit wholesalers and get your email on their buyer list. While not every deal they send out might be a good deal, if you have 20 of them sending you deals, you should start to see opportunities.

LAW #11

Location

Everybody has heard that real estate comes down to location, location, location. Having been in the business for almost ten years and seeing thousands of deals, I think that is 100% true. Nonetheless, there are some things you should keep in mind. You can still do well in a not so great location and do poorly in a perfect location; it's all about your exit strategy and timing.

I don't remember where I heard this quote, but I love it. "It's better to buy a shithole in the best neighborhood than a castle in no-where-land." Let's take a look at two different exit strategies: buy and hold for the long-term and short-term flipping. If you plan on holding on to a property for a while, then the location is of supreme importance if you care about your resale value and want to see appreciation.

I see it happen over and over again that someone buys the perfect house on five acres 45 minutes outside of the city only to find it's worth the same or even less ten years later. The other person who bought the beat-up little two-bedroom rowhouse in the up-and-coming part of the city just minutes from everything might have their property double or triple in value.

With short-term flipping, location is always a good thing to have but a little less important. Let's say you are not in the best area or maybe you are in an area far away from the city. As long as there are comps that support you purchasing the property at a certain price and selling it at a significantly higher price, you should still do the deal.

With flips, you should never buy a property for appreciation. You are forcing the appreciation by purchasing it at a discounted rate and then fixing it up and bringing it up to the market level. There are factors to take into consideration, such as holding time with less than ideal neighborhoods, but location matters a little bit less with short-term flips.

Overall, if you are buying with the plan to hold on for several years and you want to see your property value increase, then focusing on a primo location is a good idea. Do research on neighborhoods in or very close to the core city area. Or better yet, look to see if there is already a Whole Foods in the neighborhood or if they plan on putting one in. If you look up the Whole Foods effect, you'll see what I'm talking about.

Properties next to Whole Foods tend to appreciate significantly more than others. This upscale grocery chain does an immense amount of research on the developing neighborhoods, so I would recommend relying on their research. However, if you are doing a short-term flip, you can still do very well in a not so great location.

With flipping, you should never put neighborhood appreciation into your equation. So as long as there are renovated comps that have sold in the less than ideal neighborhood, you can still purchase properties there, provided you factor in that you are just bringing the property up to the market value and not expecting it to go up at all.

LAW #12

Motivated Sellers

One of the best negotiation strategies that will save you a ton of time and headaches is only negotiating with motivated sellers. It sounds obvious, but when you're getting started, you can beat yourself up and think you are a terrible negotiator for not getting the seller down on price when they are completely unrealistic. A big part of negotiating is only finding the cream of the crop or, in other words, motivated sellers to negotiate with.

The entire real estate investing business circles around buying houses from motivated sellers. To take that a step further, a motivated seller is only a small percent of the leads you are looking at.

Most leads are not motivated sellers, and you should not negotiate with most sellers. You should keep in your CRM to follow up with them a month, three months, or a year down the road because levels of motivation always change.

However, if a seller calls me and says they are thinking about selling their house for a million dollars, they want to sell six months down the road, and they are just curious what we could offer them, that is not a motivated seller. It is literally the opposite of a motivated seller. Unless it's an unusual circumstance, I would never try to negotiate to buy that property. I might try to refer it to an agent, but that seller is very far away from where you need to be to make any deal work.

A motivated seller is someone that will call you and say, "I want to sell ASAP and the house needs a lot of work." As long as they are motivated, it does not matter what price they are looking for; I would go out there and make them an offer in person or at least over the phone. A motivated seller is significantly more open to negotiating than other sellers.

Overall, when evaluating leads that are coming

into your business, you need to keep track of levels of motivation. Most sellers are not that motivated. That's okay; you can keep them in your database and follow up with them down the road, or if you just want to use them for practice negotiating, that's fine too.

You save a ton of time by only negotiating with the one in 10 leads or so that raise their hand and say they need to sell ASAP and the property needs work. The best negotiator in the world with all the negotiating techniques known to mankind won't be able to make a non-motivated seller suddenly become motivated and drop their price significantly.

LAW #13

Become An Expert

As an investor, you must be well-versed in the landlord laws of your area. They vary drastically from state to state or even county to county. I live in an area where one state is one of the most tenant-friendly states in the US, where the tenant could go several years without paying rent, and just next door, the other state is one of the most landlord-friendly states in the US.

You need to become an expert in landlord laws in your area, which means spending some time reading every article you can find online, from the actual laws to different newspaper reports, to various lawsuits between tenants and landlords, to anything else.

You will come across properties as an investor that might be occupied and will have to make the right decisions about becoming a landlord or not. I have bought houses with tenants in them and have dealt with other landlord issues, but there are some specific areas for which you could not pay me to buy a house with a tenant in it.

When buying a house with a tenant or when considering renting out a property, you need to understand the best-case and worst-case scenarios as a landlord. I'll give you a couple of quick case studies. I was evaluating a wholesale deal that still had a year-long lease on it. The property had been fixed up, it was rented at $1800 a month, and the seller only wanted 85K.

This was a good deal for a landlord but even better, if the investor did not want to be a landlord, he could wait for their lease to expire and then still make a good profit by selling it closer to 130K or 140K. Or he could keep renting it out for a large cash flow. Both options were good. This particular state also has landlord-friendly rental laws in the unlikely event there is some conflict with the tenant.

However, the one thing to keep in mind with this state, and most states, is that you need a rental license to be a legitimate rental. If you don't have a rental license, the tenant could get away with just about everything, and you would still have no recourse.

In another particular state, I was evaluating a deal where the tenant is always given the first option to purchase a property. Even if they don't want to buy the house or don't have the funds to buy the property, they can assign their rights to another buyer for a large fee, which can delay the sale for months on end.

Because the landlord laws are so antiquated and complicated in this particular jurisdiction, it's best to study up as much as possible by reading articles and the laws online as well as hiring a real estate attorney if needed.

Overall, you must become an expert in your area's tenant and landlord laws. There are a couple of things you can do to become more well-versed in this topic. For starters, you need to research on Google and YouTube everything you possibly can about being a landlord in your area, the nightmare stories as well as the success stories.

You can even visit your landlord and tenant court and sit in on some of the hearings. Anybody can go to these hearings and get a real-world education in a short period of time. Lastly, keep in mind that each state – and in some cases, each county – has drastically different laws and procedures, so always err on the conservative side, do your research, and hire a landlord lawyer if you need to get through a complicated deal.

———◆———

Entities

You need to protect yourself as a real estate investor. One of the best ways to do this is to purchase properties in some type of entity. That could be an LLC, corporation, trust, or other structure because you will be opening yourself up to a lot of unnecessary risk by purchasing the property in your own name. I am not a lawyer or CPA and not giving you legal or tax advice, but in my personal experience, the most successful real estate investors are typically not out there buying houses in their own names.

The type of entity you set up to purchase properties varies depending on what kind of deals you are doing, your level of risk, preferences, and more, but the majority of investors purchases properties in LLCs. An LLC gives you a certain level of protection and separation from your personal name and can be set up online in most states.

The reasons for purchasing properties in an LLC, trust, or even a corporation include legal protection, privacy, tax savings, and more. While an LLC won't protect you from potential legal issues, it can protect you more than if a property was in your personal name. Many investors think of LLCs, trusts, or corporations as a shield of sorts to separate their business from their personal life.

When it comes to privacy, an LLC or corporation can also be a great idea since you can set up the business anonymously and people won't be able to find out who the personal owner is in the tax records.

Many times, celebrities, wealthy investors, or people who don't want to be searched in the tax records purchase properties in an entity for this reason. Lastly, there are countless tax benefits that vary depending on what type of entity you set up. Always talk to your CPA. Having an entity for tax purposes is one of the main reasons investors purchase properties in an entity.

Overall, your level of savviness as a real estate investor regarding entities and business structures should be evolving every year. Maybe you start an LLC in your first year, read books and attend seminars on more sophisticated investing strategies with entities in your second year and set up an umbrella corporation that covers all of your real estate investing.

Every year you should be improving your knowledge, talking with CPAs, and talking with other investors to choose the right type of entity set up for your properties. There is a ton of opportunity to save money, protect assets, and more that most investors are not even aware of.

Active Versus Passive

One of the best parts of real estate investing is that there are so many different strategies and niches within the real estate investing field. If you are more hands-on, you can do rehabs; if you prefer marketing, you can do wholesaling; or if you have a lot of money and you want to be completely passive, there are numerous opportunities for that as well. You can be a private lender for established investors, own turnkey rentals, or passively invest in real estate crowdfunding or REITs.

One of the best ways to passively invest in real estate is through private lending in the first position to established investors, where your funds are secured by the property. You are essentially cutting out the bank for the investor and can make a great double-digit rate of return, while saving your investor money from using a commercial-type loan.

There are specifications within each state and for each deal, so always make sure to have a real estate lawyer look at any note. This strategy is very common and great for someone with money to lend who does not want to be involved in the day-to-day of fixing up a house and knows an investor with an established track record and good reputation.

Another passive income strategy, where you don't need nearly that much money, is buying turnkey rental properties. There are companies in areas like Memphis, Jacksonville, Dallas, and others where the company will renovate, rent, and manage properties for you in the price ranges of 80K-120K.

If you have a full-time job, this can be a great way to start making passive income to eventually build up a portfolio that you could quit your job with. Unlike traditional real estate investing, you don't have to be a property manager; in theory, all you do is collect a check every month.

Finally, another passive income strategy is putting money into REITs or real estate crowdfunding. With this last strategy, you can begin with as little as $500 and start seeing passive income on properties across the country. Overall, there are several passive income strategies when it comes to real estate investing, depending on your interests and goals.

Overall, the things to remember with all of these strategies is to do further research to see which passive income strategy is right for you. For example, private lending is only good if you have a lot of funds available and can find a trustworthy and, ideally, local investor for whom you can fund deals.

Buying turnkey rentals is excellent if you can find the right turnkey companies with a track record. There are many turnkey companies out there that might promise you the world, but some lack the property management to make the investment work. I would recommend Memphis Invest or Jacksonville Wealth Builders if you are just getting started with turnkey rentals.

Lastly, with crowdfunding and REITs, there are countless properties you can invest in that offer different levels of returns and varying amounts of risk. Overall though, after doing your research, you can be a completely passive income real estate investor using any of those strategies. You can keep your job to build your passive income stream until you can eventually quit and do investing full-time.

LAW #16

Mini-Biographies

You should try to listen to as many interviews or, as I like to call them, mini-biographies of real estate investors as possible. They are countless free YouTube interviews, podcast interviews, and more that tell you exactly how people became real estate investors, their struggles, their marketing strategies, the type of real estate investing they are doing, and their goals for the future. This will help jumpstart your business and give you tons of new ideas to implement in your own real estate investing while showing you what's possible.

If you are against spending thousands of dollars for a seminar or coaching, you could do lock yourself in your house for a weekend and listen to as many real estate investing interviews as possible while taking notes. Most people are not aware that there is an actual repeatable, predictable business model behind house flipping. They think it's just some type of investing where people get lucky now and then or that it can only be done in a good economy.

You will be amazed at how much you can learn by listening to interviews with real estate investors. Maybe you will learn that some investors are sending out 10,000 postcards a month or using a combination of exit strategies, including rehabbing and wholesaling, or how to build a team, or countless other things.

The idea with these interviews is that you will see that everyday people can become successful in real estate and that you can model many of their ideas in your own business.

Overall, you don't know what you don't know. Many beginner real estate investors have opinions on real estate investing that are shaped by the media, people close to them, real estate agents, and other people that are not out there investing in real estate and should not be listened to.

Fortunately, there are tons of free resources that allow you to listen to countless real estate investors discuss their journey of becoming successful. Your goal should be to follow the path of these real estate investors and ignore pretty much anyone else. By exposing yourself to so many ideas from so many different investors, you will start to develop your own style and brand of real estate investing.

LAW #17

—◆——◆—

Don't Quit Your Job Yet

In real estate investing, cash flow is king. One mistake I made that I hope you don't make is quitting your job too soon. Having a full- or part-time job while building a real estate investing career is not only practical, but I would actually recommend it. You will have the cash flow from your job to help pay for your marketing to find deals and, better yet, if you can get a related real estate job, then you gain valuable experience while making money.

Too many people quit their job before they've even gotten a lead or done a deal before, which is a complete mistake. Real estate investing can be a somewhat lonely business since you are doing it all by yourself and most people will tell you that it's not a good idea.

From both a financial perspective and the general socialization aspect, you should keep a job until you are 100% certain you can quit, which we will get into in this section.

When I was getting started in the business, I got a fantastic deal under contract, an easy 75K profit on a relatively small-scale deal. I was working at the time, but as soon as I got it under contract, I quit the job and thus my cash flow.

As a result, not only did I not have money for marketing to find more deals, but the deal took much longer than was expected. It dragged out for about six months, and I ended up making a bit less than expected.

During those six months, if I had kept the job, I would have been finding more deals and probably would have gotten several more properties under contract. Nowadays, there are plenty of part-time jobs in the real estate industry that you can do which can offer you real estate experience and, of course, a steady income. Many real estate investors might also be full-time agents or have another business that provides steady cash flow.

Overall, as a new real estate investor, you should be trying to build your resources and skills as much as possible. A way to do that is having a job in the real estate industry so you can have money for your marketing and business expenses. You can easily do one or two properties a month while having a full- or part-time job.

Make sure that, when the time does come to quit your job, you've completed a minimum of three deals and you have built a solid foundation of resources of at least six months' income so that you don't have to go back into the workforce. Sometimes investors can get lucky with their first deal, which is not a bad thing, but you need to have more reference experiences than just one deal before jumping into being a real estate investor.

LAW #18

───◆────◆───

War Zones

Buying houses in war zones can be tempting because of how inexpensive the property is. War zones are those areas that are not traditionally known as great neighborhoods but where the properties are dirt-cheap. In other words, these are the most notorious and least expensive areas in your city.

However, you still need to do all of your standard due diligence; in fact, even more on a war zone property. Properties in those areas take longer to sell if they sell at all, generally have no appreciation, and can be the target of burglaries and more.

When I was getting started in real estate

investing, I looked at properties that literally cost 5K because that was all I could afford at the time. I didn't know the neighborhood, and I didn't run comps. All I knew was that if a house could be bought at 5K, then it must be a good deal because it's so cheap. This type of thinking is completely wrong, and fortunately, I did not end up buying any of these houses.

You can find good deals in war zones, but you need to understand a few things. Just because you can buy a property at 5K does not mean it's a deal; you need to have actual renovated comps that have sold for 100K or 200K. Many investors make that mistake when getting started. Upon further due diligence, I realized all the properties in this particular neighborhood sold for 5K and for me to get a good deal, I would essentially have to get the property for free.

Upon even further due diligence, even getting the property for free might not have been worth it, as this was a declining neighborhood and there were not really any comps that would justify paying anything for these properties unless you could find a rehabber that you could wholesale to. Now, if there were renovated comparable sales, I might take a closer look and factor into my costs the higher the likelihood that the property would sit on the market for a while.

Overall, when buying in war zones, you need to be sure you are getting a good deal. Always check the renovated comps and what the investors are paying for these properties. Look on Zillow or Redfin in the tax record to see what investors pay for fixer-uppers in these areas.

There should be a trend of a general number that people pay for fixer-uppers in that area. Just remember that a cheap house isn't always a good deal if there are not several renovated comps at a much higher price to support that price.

Build A Dream Team

Real estate investing is a team sport, so you should look to build a team with every professional in the business, including wholesalers, title companies, lenders, real estate agents, other investors, contractors, and more. Instead of relying on one of each of these, you should strategically build a dream team where you have multiple options for each of these professionals. Having various options will give you an advantage since each title company, lender, agent, or wholesaler might offer different value and services.

One of the biggest mistakes I made when I first got started in investing was relying on one person or company for different services. Instead of relying on one person or company, you need to build a continually evolving dream team of real estate investing professionals. For example, if you are looking to find a deal through a wholesaler, you should make a list of 100 wholesalers who can send you deals instead of just the one you met down at the local REIA.

One way to do this is through LinkedIn. Type in "wholesaler" and then click on your city. Another way is finding real estate investing Facebook groups, networking at REIAs (Real Estate Investor Associations), or just writing down the phone numbers from the We Buy Houses signs on the side of the road. One wholesaler might not bring you a deal, but if you have 100 or even 25, chances are, you will find some deals.

The same is true with real estate agents. Try to reach out to hundreds of them and get them searching for deals for you, instead of relying on your cousin who just got his license. Title companies are another service where you should always be asking for referrals, checking fees, and making sure they are investor-friendly.

Lenders are another big one. If you have one lender who demands a 20-percent interest rate as an example, by building a group of 10-20 lenders, you can get the best rates and have investors fighting for your deals. Hard money lenders and private money lenders all have different rates and terms.

Overall, if you want to be successful in the business over the long term, you need to build a dream team of real estate investing professionals and think on a large scale. Instead of working with one wholesaler or real estate agent, work with 50 or 100 of each.

Instead of relying on your one lender, try to build a vast network of lenders that might offer better rates and more flexibility. Instead of relying on the one title company you have always used, try out a new one that another investor recommended to you, to make sure you are getting the best service. Keep a database of the best service providers and players on your team.

LAW #20

Practical Skillset

I was listening to business mogul Dan Kennedy the other day, who was saying there is something the majority of people don't understand, but that his renegade millionaire clients do. Becoming a millionaire or in this case, learning how to invest in real estate and build wealth is a skill set that can be learned the same way you can learn how to fix a car's transmission.

Most people think that real estate investing is a complicated skill set for which you need a real estate degree from an Ivy League school, but in reality, some of the most successful real estate investors come from blue collar backgrounds.

Real estate investing is a very practical skill set.

One of the most successful real estate investors of our time, Ron Legrand, was a struggling auto mechanic when he saw an ad about getting rich in real estate. He took the seminar, started flipping houses, and is now a millionaire many times over. How many other car mechanics saw that ad that same day, did nothing, and were in the same position a year later?

Learning how to invest in real estate is really just learning how to generate leads from motivated sellers and then choosing the cream of the crop leads from your marketing efforts. There are countless examples of people with no real estate background becoming successful after being unfulfilled with their previous job.

Overall, what you will realize about many successful real estate investors is that they are ordinary people who took action. Just like any business, there will be ups and downs, but if you find yourself a mentor, follow their strategies, and take action, you will carve out your own space for yourself as a real estate investor.

Don't for a minute think that you need to have a fancy master's degree or come from a prestigious background to be successful in real estate investing. Anybody can learn real estate investing. Once you do your first deal or two, you will see the immense potential for deals all over your city.

———◦———◦———

Stay Away From Auctions

One of the most common ways in which new real estate investors think they can get deals is down at the courthouse steps at the auction. Now, if you have never been to an auction, I would recommend you go, because they are fascinating to watch and you can learn a thing or two about how the investment business works.

That being said, I would stay away from buying auction properties unless it is an unusual circumstance, such as your neighbor's house being auctioned off, or unless you have some extreme advantage.

Going to an auction to buy properties is one of those things that sound like a great idea, but in reality, the best deals are typically not found at auction. I think you can get slightly discounted properties for the sole reason that there are not as many people at the auction as on the MLS, but you typically won't find the massive discounts that you can with off-market properties.

When bidding on an auction property, you need to know that you won't have an opportunity to look inside the house you are bidding on. In the majority of cases at the auction, the properties will go back to the bank because they have a minimum set price. There are a couple of other things you should know about auctions.

The top investors in any market are not buying at auctions. That right there should tell you something. I always try to model and emulate investors that are one, three, five, or 10 years ahead of me, and I can tell you that the most successful investors do not buy at auctions. Lastly, the legendary billionaire Charlie Munger had a famous speech about why you should avoid auctions.

He said that an "auction is just made to turn the brain into mush: you've got social proof, the other guy is bidding, you get reciprocation tendency, you get deprival super-reaction syndrome, the thing is going the other way... I mean, it just absolutely is designed to manipulate people into idiotic behavior."

Overall, what you need to know about auctions is that there are some significant disadvantages when bidding on properties. You won't be able to see the properties, the bank takes back the majority of the houses, and you have to pay cash and put down a large deposit if your offer gets accepted.

Not only that, but you never see the top investors at an auction. The top investors have usually tested all the marketing strategies out there and if they are avoiding the auctions, then you should too. Lastly, follow the wise words of billionaire Charlie Munger, who basically says that auctions turn into a feeding frenzy and manipulate you into paying more. Now, auctions are great if you are the seller, but if you are looking to buy investment properties this way, I would stay as far away as possible.

Apps And Technology

The apps and technology are always changing, but use them to your advantage as a real estate investor and be on the lookout for additional apps and new technology to help your investing. Nowadays, there are plenty of technology resources that you should utilize as a real estate investor; you don't need to try to reinvent the wheel.

Every real estate investor should be using at least several apps or programs to help them better run their business and save time. In this section, I will go over a couple of my favorite apps and programs that should give you an extra edge in real estate investing.

One of my favorite apps is Audible, which you might be using to listen to this book right now. It's great because you can learn in your car in between appointments, and you can listen to books on 1.5 X, 2 X, or even 3 X speed. You could get through at least one book a week just listening to Audible for a little bit each day in your spare time. The accumulation of that over the course of a year would probably have a significant effect on your personal development and business.

Another resource I recommend for every real estate investor is a virtual assistant. There are many places to find one, although I prefer to use Upwork, where I can get a quality and affordable virtual assistant. A virtual assistant will save you hours – if not days – in any given week. They can do things like research courthouse records for motivated sellers, edit your YouTube videos or content, post ads on Craigslist, research competitors, and countless other items.

The next thing I would recommend is using a CRM or customer relationship manager to keep track of all your prospects or anyone involved in your business. If you are serious about being a real estate investor, you need to move on from your old Excel spreadsheet and use a formal system for managing contacts and follow-up. There are plenty of free CRMs, as well as expensive CRMs, that all offer different options. I would recommend looking into Infusionsoft or Salesforce, although countless others do a great job as well.

Another great app I recommend is the Redfin app, which is free to download and will give you MLS-like access to all of the previous sales, current sales, photos, and plenty of additional information. When you are on the road and might not have access to your laptop to run comps, using Redfin can give you a good idea of the neighborhood sales.

One of my favorite tools as a real estate investor is the app Genius Scan, where you can take a picture on your cell phone and turn it into a PDF. This is essentially a mobile scanner, which is perfect for contracts.

Lastly, every real estate investor should be using the Dropbox app to access property files quickly and easily on their phone. Instead of having to dig through emails, you can just open the property file and have all of your documents uploaded into a specific property folder. I can't tell you how much time and headache this one app has saved me over the last couple of years.

Keep in mind, there are many other apps and technologies out there, and this field is always changing, so try to stay updated on what the top investors are using. You should do your own research and try to use at least five apps, pieces of software, or technologies for real estate investors.

Maybe you could make a list of the top 25 tools for real estate investors and spend a couple of weeks trying out all of them and then only keeping the top five or so that you like. I gave you the top five I like to use, but each investor has their preferences, so find out what works for you.

Don't Care What
Others Think

Legendary marketer Dan Kennedy has a famous saying: "With your marketing, if you haven't offended someone by noon every day, then you are not doing enough marketing." Most real estate investors don't do enough marketing or are scared of what others may think or say. If you want to be successful, you need to ignore all of those thoughts and think on a massive scale when it comes to lead generation. You will always have naysayers, as well as sellers that might not want to sell today.

To put things in perspective, some of the top

residential real estate investors in the US spend one million dollars a year just on marketing. Think about that for a second the next time you are doing your marketing and worry about possibly getting an angry caller. Do you think these investors are worried about offending a couple of people?

Of course not, they are focused on generating so many leads that they can cherry-pick the best deals in their market and not worried about the one percent of callers who might not be thrilled with their marketing. I know one investor who even saves any emails or phone calls from people that are mad at his marketing, kind of like a hall of fame for crazy sellers.

You should not be affected by someone who's mad at your marketing or who gives you their negative opinion on the real estate investing business. In fact, when I was getting started, I was thrilled when anyone called me because that meant my marketing was going out there.

Eventually, with my marketing, I was getting so many leads that I hired a professional call-answering service to screen any of my leads. This will save you a ton of time when you get to the point where you can hire a service or an acquisitions person. You want to do this as soon as you can so that you can focus on generating more leads and sending them into your call funnel.

When you are starting your investing business and doing marketing, you will get good leads, bad leads, and people saying the business does not work. You shouldn't put too much weight into the naysayers or ever be too worried about an angry caller.

Also, you should be doing so much lead generation and marketing that you are offending someone by noon every day. The best real estate investors get the largest number of leads, both good and bad. Don't focus on the small percentage of angry sellers or naysayers; instead, focus on your overall lead generation strategy and how to get more and more leads. Once you start taking massive action in any endeavor, you will always have detractors.

———◆———

Never Do A Deal Just
To Stay Busy

It is okay to pass on a deal in real estate investing, as there will always be another deal coming around. In fact, sometimes the best deal is the deal that you don't buy. If you are unsure or feel hesitant, you can run your deal by your hard money lender or another investor, but don't feel pressured into buying a deal you are not sure of. Part of being a successful real estate investor is passing up on 95% of the leads that come across your desk. When you buy a deal, you need to be sure that it meets all of your criteria.

Let me tell you a story about a local house-buying

company that I worked with before. They were very well-funded and could buy 20 houses a month if they chose to. I met with their CEO at one point and even wholesaled them a deal or two. He told me that many times, they just bought houses to keep their guys busy. I was completely shocked that someone would casually buy homes to keep their workers busy without properly qualifying the deal.

Even though I was new to real estate investing, it was blazingly obvious to me that this company would not last long. Fast-forward five years and, to nobody's surprise, that company is no longer in business. Buying houses just to keep someone busy is not a viable strategy and never will be.

When you buy a house as an investment, you need to choose the 1% of investment deals out there. You should have a proper vetting process, such as the MAO formula. The most successful investors get a ton of leads and then only put under contract a tiny percent of their leads.

Some local investors I know just do one or two deals a year, but because their criteria for buying houses are so strict, those one or two deals a year do significantly better than the investor casually purchasing a home or two each month to keep their guys busy.

Overall, when it comes to real estate investing, you should focus more on the quality of the deal than the quantity. You need to properly evaluate every single deal and make sure that the deal is a winner before purchasing.

If you are new to real estate investing, you can always ask your local hard money lender or another investor you know, like, and trust to tell you whether it's a good deal. Be very selective about the deals you buy and never buy a house to keep someone busy. That is one of the fastest ways I know to go out of business.

Stay Away From Weird Houses

Stay away from the weird houses if you are new to the business. They may be significantly lower priced than other houses, but if there are no other similarly weird houses that have sold, then you have nothing to compare the house to. Weird homes sit on the market longer, sell for much lower, and the overall pool of people looking to buy or rent a weird house is much smaller. They are high-risk and, unless you are an experienced investor, you should avoid them at all costs.

What exactly is a weird house? A couple of examples of weird houses are an 800-square-foot house in a neighborhood of 2500-square-foot homes. Or a house in front of a fire station on a busy corner, or a house in tear-down condition, or a house with just two bedrooms in a neighborhood of four-bedroom homes. These houses don't have many – if any – comparable sales, and it is challenging to predict the after renovated sales price.

It can be tempting to buy these houses because of how much lower they are in comparison to the neighborhood, but you should avoid them when starting out. I would never buy a house unless I have two or three comps of the exact same or similar property being sold within the last year. If you are unsure of the property being a weird house or not, ask your local hard money lender or any investor you know, like, and trust. They can usually tell you fairly quickly what they think about the deal.

Overall, stick to what you know with real estate investing. It is safer and more predictable. Don't just buy a house because it is at a lower price. There are numerous variables with weird houses that you might not see coming. For example, the house might have to be torn down, or it might sell for the price of a condo because of its size.

If you do end up buying a weird house, be very, very, very conservative with your numbers and always run it by someone you know, like, and trust before buying. If you are a more experienced investor, you can look at these so-called weird houses and do things like adding on additions, building new construction, or other advanced strategies. However, as a beginner, I would stay away.

LAW #26

Learn Tax Laws

Real estate investing has significant tax implications. Just a few tweaks in your investing strategy can have an impact of tens or even hundreds of thousands of dollars. I would almost always recommend that you hire a qualified CPA, but at the same time, you should be learning the ins and outs of your tax laws. There are plenty of seminars, online classes, and books that can give you the edge as a real estate investor.

When you are first getting started, at the very least, you should have some type of tax system for your real estate investing. I recommend doing several things. You should sign up for QuickBooks online to track your business, hire a

CPA, and educate yourself as much as humanly possible on tax info. By becoming an expert in the tax laws in your area, you will have a considerable advantage over other investors.

There are plenty of seminars and classes you should be taking as a real estate entrepreneur when it comes to doing your taxes. One investor I know was taking online personal development classes on tax laws so that he could gain an edge over other investors. What I would not recommend is doing everything yourself to save a couple of hundred bucks.

You need a bulletproof system when it comes to taxes and have at the very least a basic understanding of the implications, depending on the type of real estate investing you are doing. As you grow as a real estate investor and build your real estate empire, your taxes will get more and more complicated, and you need to have the right professionals working for you.

Overall, when it comes to taxes, you should have several levels of safety nets. The first thing you should do at the very least is sign up for QuickBooks and/or another tax accounting program.

Next, you should interview or research the best CPAs in your area that have experience working with real estate investors and entrepreneurs. Lastly, you should educate yourself as much as possible on the tax laws through books, seminars, and classes. Every year, your tax strategy should be evolving as you become a more experienced and savvier investor.

LAW #27

Build Systems

If you want to be a successful real estate investor, you must become great at delegating tasks and creating repeatable systems. You need to think of building a team, but that does not mean you need to hire full-time staff or anything like that.

Much of the real estate investing business can be outsourced to virtual assistants so that they can do the majority of the work for you. Nowadays, it is easy and inexpensive to delegate tasks to professional assistants. I will go over a couple of standard business systems you should outsource, although you could really outsource anything.

As a real estate investor, you should think of yourself as a lead generation company with, ideally, tons of leads coming in on a regular basis. Since most of these leads are not great, it is not worth your time to sift through, qualify, and answer all of the phone calls.

Fortunately for you, there are plenty of professional call-answering services whose staff answer your calls and fill out your seller lead sheet for a couple of hundred dollars a month. Some of these services include PAT Live, AnswerFirst, Dedicated Office Systems, and plenty of other great ones.

Another system you should outsource is your list building. When I was first getting started, I physically went down to the courthouse to pull lists of motivated sellers or drove all around town to take note of distressed properties. While I got excellent lists, it was not the greatest use of my time.

Fortunately, there are plenty of great list providers out there that have already done the work of compiling the lists, such as Alesco Data, Melissa Data, List Source, and many others. If you would prefer to get the data directly from the courthouse, many courthouses now have all of their data online. You just have to subscribe to the land records at your county's website, and you can gain access.

Lastly, you should outsource your marketing, especially direct mail. I think direct mail is still by far the best source of leads, although it's not worth your time to be handwriting and sending out the letters yourself. Once again, there are countless direct mail fulfillment services, such as click2mail.com and many others. All you have to do is upload your list of motivated sellers, and they will send out your postcards or letters. This will save you hours of handwriting letters. Ask me how I know.

Overall, you need to be smart with your time as a real estate investor. By outsourcing the three aforementioned systems, you can be up and running in no time. Keep in mind that in many cities all you need is one deal per year to make six figures or do very well, so put time into building your system and be patient with it.

The business is all about lead generation, and your goal should be to funnel as many leads as possible to your acquisitions or call-answering service and then only follow up with the most motivated ones. You could even have a full-time job while doing all of this because once this system is set up, it will take maybe 30 minutes a week to run it effectively.

Be Prepared And Move Fast

I could easily make this law #1, but in real estate investing you have to move fast. The best deals from motivated sellers do not last very long as other investors out there are trying to get the same deals. When you find a motivated seller and a good deal, you must go out there on the same day, if possible, and get the property under contract. I have lost several deals as a result of taking my time and get several other deals by moving faster than the next investor.

During the first couple of months of my real estate investing career, I came across an amazing deal in a great neighborhood. The seller called me on the weekend, leaving a voicemail about the property, the price he was looking for, and that he wanted to sell ASAP. I was thrilled, and I planned on calling him first thing the next day on Monday morning.

However, by the time I called him back, he told me he had already gone with another investor who had met him out there on Sunday. I was completely disappointed. If I had only called this guy back and met him, I could have made more in one deal than I had been making at my job all year.

Another lesson I learned was from a seller who called me over the weekend and wanted to sell ASAP without any commissions. I was not going to make the same mistake twice, so this time I spoke with her and made her an offer over the phone, which she agreed to. I told her I would send over the offer for electronic signatures and we would be ratified. She seemed a little hesitant with the electronic signature since I had not technically met her in person, but I didn't think much of it because she had still agreed to sign it.

I sent over for e-signing on a Sunday but didn't see that she had signed it. The next day I saw that the property was listed on the market with a real estate agent and under contract. Most likely, it went to another cash buyer who had actually met the seller at the property. If only I had gone to meet them in person, that would have made the difference.

To wrap this story up, I finally did learn my lesson. I got a call from a motivated seller who told me I had contacted him a year ago about selling his house, but now he really wanted to sell. The house was in the perfect area and was smaller, so it didn't need a ton of work.

He told me I had about 30 minutes before he was leaving for the weekend, so I spent five minutes running comps, drove there as fast as I could, and put the property under contract, which ultimately led to a close with six-figure profit.

Overall, ultimately, you always need to be prepared to make a deal and move as fast as possible when you have a motivated seller. Keep in mind that most sellers are not motivated, but the five to 10% of your leads that are motivated will keep calling other investors until someone gives them exactly what they need – a fast offer today.

Do not delay on making offers or meeting people in person. Always have a folder of printed-out contracts in your car ready to go and spend any time you have getting to know different neighborhoods so it can help you with your comps. I have learned my lesson and hope you don't make the same mistake.

LAW #29

Ignore Naysayers

When getting into real estate investing, you have to ignore just about everybody who gives you advice. They usually fall into one of two categories: people who failed at real estate investing at one point in their career, and people who never had the guts to take any risks and don't want to see you succeed. I can't tell you how many people discouraged me from doing real estate investing and still do to this day.

Keep in mind, the general public is wrong about just about everything, including real estate investing. The majority of people are wrong about fitness as they are not in shape; wrong about wealth building as they are not wealthy, and wrong about career advice since most of them hate their jobs.

When I was getting into real estate, several people told me it could not or should not be done. These are the people that appear anytime you try to start any type of business or take any risk that might threaten their fragile mindset. The first type of person, like I mentioned, has failed before and gave up on their dreams.

When I was first getting started, I had a real estate agent who could list 100 reasons why people should not invest in real estate. The only problem was that this obviously was not a full-time real estate investor, and the only properties that he had bought had lost money. He never really had a strategy for real estate investing and, as a result, got unlucky on a few deals.

Hence, he now preaches why real estate investing is bad. This is the first type of person you should avoid – someone in the industry who might have tried and failed. When getting advice on anything, you should only look at the successful people in their respective industries, not the people who gave up.

The next type of person is the person who is too smart for their own good and never really took any risks. I had a professor like this, who had never started a business and never worked for a business, yet somehow was teaching business. It never made much sense to me and I didn't listen to my professors much anyways, but this person was giving business advice as if it was an absolute fact.

Their idea of starting a business was spending three months writing a business plan, spending another three months analyzing the market to find competitors, and then spending yet another three months talking with potential investors about raising money. In the real world of business and real estate investing, that's not how it works.

There are full-time investors in every market in the US who do things differently. They jump into their market, start marketing, find deals, grow their business, and carve out their own niche regardless of how many other investors there are.

Overall, when you are getting real estate investing advice, you have to seek out the 1% of investors out there who are consistently doing deals and have made a profession out of it. If you were trying to become a world-class cook, would you listen to people who couldn't make a grilled cheese sandwich or would you try to get advice from world-class professionals?

Real estate investing is similar and fortunately, there are countless places – both free and paid – where you can get advice directly from full-time investors. These include interviews on podcasts and YouTube videos of full-time house flippers. If you spent a weekend listening to 50 of these interviews while taking notes, you would know exactly what to do in the real estate investing world.

There are also paid coaching programs you can join, which is what I did when getting started. Lastly, if you start marketing and bringing deals to the top investors in your local area, the top investors will often want to mentor you and help you get your first deals done since you bring them the leads. There are many ways to find the correct advice, but make sure you avoid the unsuccessful ones at all times.

Stats Lie

I took a statistics class in college. Even though I didn't do very well, I remember my professor was pretty blunt. One of his lessons has stuck with me to this day. He said you could interpret stats in almost any way you want, or in other words, stats lie and can be manipulated easily.

In real estate, this is even more common as you see different investors and agents telling you that a fixer-upper can sell for this and this price renovated, or that a property might only cost 20K to fix up – when in reality, it might be 100K – and countless other ways to manipulate the stats. Almost any stat can be completely exaggerated, and I give a wild example of just some of the nonsense you see in the real estate industry.

"Hello, Lied The Real Estate Agent..."

There is one agent in my area who claims to have sold something like 100M in his first year, to be an angel investor, to be the off-market real estate expert with thousands of houses available off market, and many other dubious claims. The interesting thing about these stats, upon a closer look, is that although incredulous, they are all technically true.

However, they are also entirely manipulated. I'll explain. The 100M in his first year would be an incredible feat; I would be shocked if anyone in the history of real estate has ever done this in their first year. The only problem with it is that these were flat fee listings. In other words, the sellers paid this service a couple of hundred dollars to get their property listed on the MLS instead of being a for sale by owner property.

This agent had no involvement with the actual sales. The seller did all the negotiation and would get the deal to closing. It was merely a service to put the property on the MLS. However, the agent represented the sales as if they were full-service listings although not surprisingly, these types of sales are no longer allowed to count for the top agent awards.

The next claim is that he is an angel investor, which probably makes you think of moving around millions of dollars in Silicon Valley. In reality, he puts money into Kickstarter campaigns. Anyone that has an account and $20 to their name can do this; however, technically speaking, it is still angel investing. It would be the same as me calling myself an international philanthropist because I just donated $50 to CharityWater.org.

Next, he says he is the off-market expert with thousands of off-market deals. What he is referring to is that on Zillow, there is a section where people say "make me move" and usually put in a pretty ridiculous price. He puts a link to these on his website to make it seem as if he is doing all of this work to dig up thousands of diamond in the rough, off-market properties. I could go on and on with pretty much every single thing in his biography, but this is all under the guise of him calling himself the "honest agent."

The key to power with this principle is that even the person calling themselves the honest one and telling you to watch out for other unscrupulous investors or agents should not be trusted. Be skeptical of stats and numbers that seem too good to be true, or better yet, you should trust but verify – just like the famous quote.

Most people are not manipulative in real estate, but some might give you a number on a property just because they don't know any better. For example, I continuously see wholesalers tell new investors that a house might only need 20K worth of work, when in fact, it requires five times that.

Or an agent might tell you that a renovated home could sell for 600K when it might only sell for 500K. Always verify your own numbers since you can see with the previous examples how easy it is to manipulate data. Use what someone else might say to you as part of the pieces to the puzzle, but never take it as absolute fact.

Multiple Sources Of Funding

When it comes to funding your real estate deal, you should never rely on one source. Many investors might depend on the one hard money lender they met at a convention two years ago without exploring all of the financing options available. Nowadays, there is an ever-expanding pool of money to tap into for your real estate deals.

You have hard money, conventional financing, private money, partnerships, crowdfunding, and more. If you are doing just five or 10 deals a year and you find a source of funding that can save you a point or a couple of percent, that could literally save you $100,000 per year.

As an investor, you should evaluate numerous hard money lenders since they all offer slightly different rates and evaluate numerous other sources of financing. It's better to have several sources lined up than to rely on just one, and that goes for everything in real estate investing, including working with real estate agents, wholesalers, and even your own lead generation efforts.

Your goal as an investor should be to consistently get your financing costs down while gaining more flexibility with your financing. For example, maybe if you pitch to enough investors, you can find private money lenders willing to do an 8% loan and close in two weeks.

Moreover, there are plenty of potential options when it comes to funding your deal online through one of the real estate crowdfunding sites. Some sources of funding might be very low-interest rates but might take 30-45 days to close, and you will have to go through lots of hurdles to make the deal happen.

Overall, you should write on a spreadsheet or document about 20 different sources of funding and the pros and cons of working with each one. By talking to three or five hard money lenders, you can see how different their rates might be and how much you might be able to save by going with a different lender. Try to do some research into financing so that you don't have to rely on the one lender you've always used.

There are multiple factors in each lender, including whether they are easy to work with, how fast they can fund, what their interest rates are, how many points they charge, what types of deals they can lend on, and more. Then when you get a deal, you can find the best lender for that deal because you've already vetted 20 of them and know exactly what they are looking for.

These days, there are so many non-traditional sources of financing that you would be crazy not to look into them. The types of funding you should look into include hard money lenders, private money from friends and family, crowdfunding, lines of credit from local banks, conventional financing, and even partnerships.

Protect Your Reputation

The real estate investing world is a small world, no matter how big or competitive you think your city may be. You will see the same people over and over again, whether they are hard money lenders, real estate agents, or other investors. Hence, you need to be sure that you have a rock-solid reputation.

Be sure that people know you are someone who can get deals done and is easy to work with. This will open up more deals and more opportunities for you and generally make doing business an easier proposition.

I will give you a couple of examples of this principle in action. In my market, and this is probably true for different markets, you meet investors of all shapes and sizes. There is one company in particular that is known for getting deals done, does a ton of marketing, and gets the job done quickly and efficiently. People know them as the go-to company if you have a house you need to sell fast, and as a result of their branding and their reputation, they get many referrals.

Professionals such as real estate agents, lenders, and others know which company to call when a house needs to be sold fast, and sellers who need to sell quickly know who to call as well. This has a snowball effect where they get more and more referrals and do tons of marketing and keep increasing the number of deals they are doing. People like doing business with them and know they will get the deal done with no drama.

On the other hand, there is an agent and quasi investor in my area who has a horrible reputation for making deals difficult and causing headaches throughout the entire transaction. As a result of this, his reputation precedes him, and people try to avoid this person like the plague.

Like I mentioned, word gets around quickly in the real estate industry. Who do you think people talk about at their real estate happy hours? Usually, the extremely difficult people who tend to be pretty far out there. As a result of his reputation, people do not want to work with him. I'm not sure how many deals he has missed out on as a result of his reputation, but I'm sure it is quite a few.

Overall, I have given you two extreme examples, but keep in mind, you must guard your reputation. Every deal you do will help you build your reputation. If you can work in a professional and easy-to-do-business-with manner, you can slowly build your reputation as a deal maker. If you screw someone over or make things miserable for someone else in the real estate investing industry, it might work once, but keep in mind that word will spread since it's such a small community. You will get more deals if you can build a rock-solid reputation.

Always Be Evolving

This principle applies to any type of business. You should always be recreating yourself and your business by staying ahead of the curve, learning new strategies, and hearing new ideas. Invest in yourself as much as possible by reading books, attending seminars in your own industry and other industries, getting mentors, and joining mastermind groups that require an application process. The real estate business is continually changing, and you need to surround yourself with excellence to make sure you stay at the top of your game.

I will give you a quick story. A couple of years ago, I was working with a real estate agent who did pretty well for himself and was making a couple of hundred thousand dollars each year. At the same time, I would attend real estate events with another real estate investor who was also doing very well and building a very successful business.

The biggest difference between these two entrepreneurs was that the agent was against any type of coaching or further learning and did not attend seminars, read books, or do any kind of networking to improve his business. And why would he? In his mind, he was already successful making several hundred thousand dollars per year, so what could he possibly have to learn from someone else?

The other entrepreneur had a different mindset and was hungry, looking for any little piece of information, book, seminar, mastermind, or anything that could give him a slight advantage. Fast-forward about three years. Can you guess the results?

The agent who was against further learning is still in the exact same position as he was before, although I know several agents have left his company. The other entrepreneur is now one of the most successful investors in the country with a real estate empire and a nationwide reach. The most significant difference is that the real estate investor had an open mindset and was looking to evolve.

Overall, a lot of people say that you will be the same person in five years as you are today except for the people you meet and the books you read. I would add to that the seminars you attend, the mastermind groups you are a part of, AND the books you read. You never know where the next piece of information that can take your business to the next level will come from.

In some cases, it might even be from an entirely different industry, which is why you should attend seminars within your own industry, but maybe a couple from other industries as well, such as marketing or technology. You will meet people at these conferences, seminars, and masterminds that can help propel you and grow your business.

———•——•——•———

Keep Things Simple

Keep things simple in real estate investing. I can't overemphasize this point enough. When working with sellers or other potential partners, remember that a confused mind says no. I've seen deals fall apart, costing in total hundreds of thousands of dollars, over making a deal unnecessarily complicated.

If you are an experienced, savvy investor, then there are more complicated and structured ways of doing deals. However, if you are new, you need to make things uncomplicated. This is especially true when working with a motivated seller. Keep in mind, they are stressed out and want to get rid of the house as soon as possible – they want the easiest solution out.

One of the best deals I did was because another investor tried to set up a joint venture with the seller instead of quickly buying the house as is. Eventually, the seller called me, frustrated that this investor was trying to set up a joint venture when they had zero interest in doing so. The investor messed up big time by trying to set up a complicated deal.

Another example of this was a lender I was going to work with. It seemed to me as if he was trying to impress upon me his knowledge of real estate because every other word out of his mouth was some complicated real estate term and structure. I tried to keep things simple and say, "Okay, so how about this percent on these terms?" To make a long story short, the message was lost in translation and again was unnecessarily complicated.

It's almost like the show *Shark Tank*, where one shark might offer 100K for 10%, while Kevin might offer them a 1% royalty over the next 10 years on purchases over 100$, 5% equity, and a $500,000 loan payback at 12% interest. I have almost never seen someone take those deals. To me, it seems like they have no idea what he's talking about. With so many variables, it's hard to gauge the actual value on the deal.

The bottom line with real estate investing is to keep things so simple that anybody could understand. The more variables you include in a deal, the more unlikely someone might accept. A motivated seller almost always wants a fast close, as is, and no real estate commission.

Anything outside of that, I would only try at your own risk. With motivated sellers, it's all about the speed and ease of the transaction. When working with partners, you can get into more complicated deals, but I would only recommend that strategy if you are experienced. If you create any confusion over a deal or can tell that another investor might not 100% understand the deal, then you can bet the answer will be no. Keep it simple and straightforward, and you will be okay.

Real Estate Masterminds

Utilize the power of real estate mastermind groups. Mastermind groups were one of the main principles Napoleon Hill talked about in *Think and Grow Rich*. Industrialists like Henry Ford, Andrew Carnegie, and countless other successful people were all in mastermind groups of some form. People always say that the closest people you associate with are who you will become.

By joining a real estate mastermind group, you can take your business to the next level. As a real estate investor, you should always be looking for advantages – even if it's only a one-percent advantage. A mastermind group is something that can have a significant impact on your business.

There are numerous reasons to join a real estate mastermind, including networking and hanging out with likeminded successful real estate investors. A good mastermind has successful investors from different cities, doing different types of deals at different price ranges, and you will have access to learn their best strategies. All of the investors go around the room talking about their business, what's been working really well, and what their challenges have been.

Not only will you learn some of the best strategies, but you will also be meeting and networking with top investors who will become friends and associates, and who will open the doors to do even more deals. I don't care how smart you are or think you are – if you don't think you can learn something from a real estate mastermind, you are crazy.

Another great thing about them is that you will be given the opportunity to talk about your own business, your successes, and your challenges, and the mastermind group will give you answers about how they overcame those challenges. Your business will grow as a result of a mastermind group, and you will grow as a person with everything you are learning and all the people you are meeting.

Overall, the thing with real estate masterminds is that they come in all shapes and sizes. Everything is called a mastermind these days, so you need to do some qualification with your mastermind. If you are just getting started in the business, then any type of mastermind is great to get a feel for the business.

However, after you start doing deals, you should try to join a mastermind that has membership criteria. You do not want to be the smartest person in the room. Some masterminds require you to be doing at least five, 10, or even 50-100 deals a year.

There is every level of mastermind out there, and the competitive nature of trying to get to the next level of a mastermind will help your business. Isolation is dangerous. If you are looking to improve your business and crush your competition, then a mastermind is a must.

Master This Skill

If you were to master one skill that would allow you to be a full-time real estate investor, it would be lead generation. Real estate investing can be thought of as a complicated business, but if you learn how to make your phone ring, you don't need to know the other complexities because you will figure them out as you go.

I can guarantee you, once you get a motivated seller lead, you will learn quickly what you need to do to get the deal done. That's what I did. I knew very little about real estate investing when I first got started, but I knew how to make my phone ring – and that was the most important thing.

There are many ways of making your phone ring with leads. One of the best is direct mail. I know it sounds old-school, but there is not a single better dollar-for-dollar marketing strategy that is as targeted as direct mail.

Whether your budget is $50 a month, like mine was when I got started, or $5000 a month, direct mail is the most scalable and profitable source of leads. When I send out a certain number of letters, I know how many calls I will get, and I know how many calls it takes to get a deal – usually about 25-50.

I believe in using multiple sources of marketing to get your leads. Moreover, you should always play to your strengths. Some of the other ways of getting deals include online marketing with pay per click, strategic networking with other investors and agents, bandit signs, canvassing neighborhoods, working the MLS, and countless other strategies.

I was just talking with my hard money lender, and I asked him how the majority of his investors that he lends money to find their deals. He told me they all have different ways of getting deals and that they started with something basic they were interested in and worked it until they were getting consistent leads.

Once you find a strategy you are interested in and you think you can make work, you'll start to see little inefficiencies in the marketing strategy to get even more and more deals. If you can master at least one strategy for finding deals, you can master real estate investing, and you will always have deals.

Overall, although there are countless ways of getting deals, direct mail is a fantastic thing, especially for someone like me, who started their business career off as a telemarketer. I used to have to call hundreds of people per day, most of whom did not want to talk to me. With direct mail, people are calling you, saying they want to sell their house. Then you just look for the motivated sellers and only work with them.

The main thing to realize with this strategy is that most people do direct mail wrong because they will mail out a minimum number of letters just one time instead of applying a three-step mailing campaign. Then they say direct mail does not work.

No matter what tactic you use for finding deals, I would start by learning how to get your first lead in a month, then your first 10 leads, then 20, and try to scale it up from there. If you learn this one skill of generating leads, you will always have deals.

LAW #37

The Economy

The economy is not as important as you think when you're investing in real estate. Newer real estate investors believe the entire real estate investing business is dependent on whether the economy is up or down. In reality, professional real estate investors are purchasing properties on margins using the MAO formula, which builds in a profit in any type of market.

Also, because you are only holding on to the property for a short time as an investor, it's not as big of a factor as you would think. If you focus your business on the ability to find discounted deals relative to the market and you're not dependent on the market to gain 10 or 20% over the course of when you buy the deal, then you are good.

Only amateur investors depend on the economy to thrive as a real estate investor. When the market does crash, they are weeded out because they are depending on the after renovated value to be significantly higher than what previous comps have sold for.

That's called speculation, and it's not what professional investors do. The smart and savvy investors who thrive in up *and* down markets are good at finding deals and never base their profits off of the economy going up or down. The reason the MAO or maximum allowable offer formula has been around for so long is that it works no matter the economy.

The most dangerous thing you can do as a short-term real estate investor is think that, because you might be in a strong economy, a renovated property that previously sold for 200K will probably sell for 220K or 225K three to six months down the road.

That is what we call speculation, and it is the

fastest way to go out of business. If you are holding on for future appreciation for five, 10, or even 15 years down the road, then that's fine, but in the short-term flipping business, you never factor in the economy.

Overall, focus your business on being able to generate off-market leads through your own marketing, networking, and systems. The investors and lenders that make it through any economy do so because they are conservative.

In many cases, they even thrive in a down market because it weeds out all of the amateur investors and there are more deals at low prices. Remember the Warren Buffet quote that you should be greedy when others are fearful and fearful when others are greedy.

LAW #38

Become A
Transaction Engineer

If you become a transaction engineer, you will never run out of deals. Ron Legrand, the legendary real estate investor, talks about this principle. It means that you can evaluate deals and while wearing any number of hats. While most investors are wholesalers or rehabbers or only buy rental properties, if you become a transaction engineer, you will be able to do a variety of deals.

That means, in a given month, you might wholesale a deal, buy a rehab, joint venture, lend on a property, buy a rental, and possibly even do a deal as a real estate agent.

The more exit strategies you have, the more deals you will be able to do point blank. If you are getting 100 leads a month but you are only looking at them through the eyes of a wholesaler, you are probably leaving a lot of money on the table.

Out of those 100 leads, some could be great to own as a rental property, rehab, wholesale, joint venture, lend money on the deal in the first position, or even be a real estate broker on the deal.

Now, when you are getting started, you should only focus on one type of transaction, but as you evolve as an investor, you should try to add more exit strategies to your arsenal. It's similar to Bruce Lee's fighting style Jeet Kun Do or, in other words, the "no way way." Depending on his opponent, he could use the best strategies from any of the fighting styles out there.

When I first got started as a real estate investor, I would only do wholesale deals because I was a little hesitant to take on rehabs. However, after passing up on lots of lucrative deals, I decided to shift my strategy to doing mostly wholesale deals but also cherry-picking the best rehab deals and wholesaling the rest.

I can also do a deal as an agent if I come across a discounted lead that does not quite meet my criteria but is still a good deal for someone that would live there and fix it up. Or another exit strategy would be something that's called wholetailing, in between a rehab and a wholesale. Essentially, you buy the property at enough of a discount where you just clean out the house, do some minor landscaping if needed, and then list it as a fixer-upper, as is property.

There are many exit strategies out there, from wholesale, rehab, buy and hold, wholetail, real estate broker deals to many more. The fastest way to increase the number of deals you are doing is to add an additional exit strategy to your war chest. Every investor has their own niche and specialty, so when you are getting started, you should focus on your strengths while looking to add more strategies.

Your goal should be to become the transaction

engineer. If you have five exit strategies instead of just one, it will make even the most competitive market seem to have an endless number of deals because you will know the highest and best use of each lead.

Many of the top investors eventually evolve their business into having different branches, such as a wholesale branch, rehab, lending, and possibly even a brokerage branch. Those are all mutually beneficial, bring in more opportunities in combination, and have a snowball effect.

LAW #39

Reward Yourself

When you complete a successful real estate investment deal, you need to go out and celebrate. Buy or do something fun. Whether you made 100K or 5K, which I have done both of, it deserves a celebration. In fact, one of my first deals was a 5K deal, and I was more thrilled with that than some of my bigger deals because it was reassurance that this business does work.

With any deal, you are celebrating the fact you've made money, but also the fact you were able to put all the variables together that go into a successful real estate deal. The best thing about completing a transaction is celebrating and taking the check to the bank, but more importantly the knowledge that you gained from the deal. Each deal you do makes you a better investor.

Real estate investing can be a roller coaster ride, so once you get to closing, it is the best feeling in the world. You should set goals for yourself after any successful deal so that you have something to look forward to in addition to any profit you might make.

Some investors I know go out to a fancy dinner, some might go to Miami for the weekend, and others might go to Europe for a month. Because this business can be profitable, I would recommend setting big rewards if you hit your goals.

You should take any money from an investment deal and put a good portion of it away for savings, a good amount for taxes, some money for marketing for additional properties, some for reinvesting in your own education, and then go ahead and blow the rest of it on something fun.

After my last big deal, I paid for live events from three of the top marketers in the world, including hanging out at one of their houses for a day. These were all in different cities, so it was an awesome time and I felt like I was on vacation as well as learning a ton and networking. There are countless ways to celebrate your real estate victories, so feel free to come up with your own.

Real estate investing is one of the most fun and exciting businesses I can think of, and I always recommend somehow celebrating a successful deal. It is also interesting and helpful to keep track of your successful deals so that you can show them to potential investors and look back to see what you learned from each deal.

Success breeds success. With each deal I do, I learn something and get better. The celebrations get better and better as well. I used to go out for a happy hour with friends. Now that the deals have gotten bigger and more consistent, I've also scaled up the adventures and post-deal celebrations.

Avoid Difficult People

The real estate industry, while it is a small community, has a lot of people. There is absolutely no reason to depend on a service or person if they are challenging to work with, negative, unlucky, unhappy, weird, or any other number of things. For example, if a real estate agent does not want to work with you and does not like investors, there are 1000 other real estate agents you could talk to.

The same goes for working with title companies, lenders, other investors, and anyone else. You want to be continually building your own real estate investing dream team and keeping note of the people you should avoid at all costs.

It's incredible to me how many investors rely on a service or person within the real estate investing industry that they don't enjoy working with. What I didn't realize when I was getting started is that there are so many providers of the service that you are looking for that you don't need to put up with any BS.

In my business, the one strike policy applies. If a person or a company is being difficult, unpleasant, weird, or any other number of things, I can go find 10 different providers of the exact same service but better.

I have worked with nightmare partners and service providers when I should have done the obvious and worked with someone else. For example, if your lender is not giving you the best rates or is being difficult, you should talk to other lenders. You should do that anyway when you are first building your team.

Make sure you have several lenders, several title companies, numerous real estate agents, many other investors, and that you are always adding to your team to see if someone can provide a better service.

Avoid at all costs people that are difficult to work with, unhappy, or weird. It will make your life and business much easier. You should start compiling lists of all the service providers within the real estate investing industry. Even make notes of who to avoid and then move others to the top of the list.

Ask for referrals from other real estate investors that you know, like, and trust. You would be surprised how many names of amazing partners and providers they will give you. You should also be testing the waters, even if you have amazing services that you are currently working with. Try doing a deal with a new provider just to see how it compares – you never know.

LAW #41

Study Your Competition

Every smart real estate investor and entrepreneur should study other real estate investors in their own market and in other markets. There is a lot to be learned – both good and bad – from your direct competition.

All it takes is one little tweak to make a large difference in your business. You should not have your head in the sand doing the same thing every single year. By keeping your mind open for new ideas from your competition and other investors, you will ensure that you don't get left behind.

Nowadays, studying your competition is fairly easy, and you would be insane not to at least look at what other investors are doing. I'm not talking about copying anybody, but what I *am* talking about is looking for new ideas and tweaks that you can make to your business.

You can follow other investors on social media, browse their websites, look at articles, and listen to their interviews. You can even browse job application sites such as Craigslist and others for the types of people they are looking to hire and how much they are paying them.

I bet if you were to pick five successful real estate investors and do all of the aforementioned things, there would be at least three amazing ideas that you could implement. You typically want to look for ideas from investors that are five to 10 years ahead of you in the business. It's almost like looking into a magic crystal ball. You could get an idea of where you would be in the next few years if you pick up the best strategy from each investor.

That's another reason why I always recommend going to real estate mastermind events. At these groups, different successful investors get up and tell everyone the best strategy that is working for them, and everyone is in a different market. You can then model the best ideas for your own company.

The best free education you can ever get is by modeling and looking for ideas from your top competition, locally as well as nationally. Every so often, at least once a quarter, you should spend several hours – if not an entire day – looking for ideas from what other real estate investors across the country and in your own backyard are doing.

If you compile a list of all the ideas and improvements you could make once a quarter and keep up this habit, then within a few years, your business will be transformed to the next level, and then the next level after that.

LAW #42

◆━━━━━◆━━━━━◆

There Is An Infinite Supply Of Deals

One of the most important things you will learn as a real estate investor is that the business really is a zero-sum game. This is what Dan Kennedy considers one of the biggest differences between his renegade millionaire clients and the general public.

Renegade millionaires get that there is an infinite supply of deals and opportunities and they have an abundance mentality. When you are getting started, it can seem as if the deals are running out. However, the top investors know that no matter how many people are investing in real estate, there will always be deals when you know how to generate leads and have a good network.

After doing my first three real estate investment deals, I had a scarcity mindset. Since they were my first couple of flips, it took me some effort to get them. I was seeing other investors buying up houses at a rapid rate, and I thought to myself, how could there possibly be any more deals out there? This was completely wrong. I soon realized that there will always be an endless number of deals, for several reasons.

First off, there will always be motivated sellers looking to sell the property fast without a real estate agent; there is nothing that will change that. Secondly, there are countless ways to partner with other investors, so even if you think there are no more deals, you could always partner with another investor who has a deal and still make a considerable profit.

For example, you could lend money to them on their deal, or if you get a property under contract and they have a massive buyer list of thousands of people, you could send it out on their list and get a premium price for the property, also known as a co-wholesale. Lastly, the top investors in any market typically train new investors on how to find deals and work out joint ventures with them. You would think that all of the deals would run out with this much competition. In fact, the opposite is true. With more competition, the top investors do even more deals.

The bottom line is, if you get your marketing right with a steady stream of leads, you will have nothing to worry about. Some of the most profitable deals I have ever done, the seller told me they received numerous other letters and postcards but decided to call me. You would think a seller would shop around 10 times, but that is often not the case.

The more leads you get, the more exit strategies you have, and the more people you know, the more certain it becomes that you will always have deals going on – no matter what the economy is doing or how competitive you think your market is. To paraphrase Richard Branson, good deals are like the bus – there is always another one coming around.

—◆———◆———◆—

Have a Follow-Up System

Every investor needs a rock solid follow-up system for prospects, potential joint venture partners, lenders, and more. If you are doing consistent marketing and not following up with sellers that have called you in the past, then I guarantee you that you are missing out on deals every year.

This goes for real estate agents you know, potential lenders, and other professionals. You need to stay at the top of their minds and catch up every so often to see what's new and whether you can be of benefit to each other.

A follow-up system for leads can be as simple as having a CRM where you put in a follow-up sequence of any lead to be contacted every month for the next year. Or to give the seller a little more time, you can make the sequence to contact them every three months until they either tell you to stop contacting them or they sell their property.

When I was getting started, I can't tell you how many deals I lost because I didn't follow up six months or a year down the road. I even saw my competition posting on social media six months later about a great deal they just bought and it had been the same seller who had originally contacted me. That will make you set up a follow-up system pretty quickly – I can guarantee you that.

Motivation levels change with sellers. Another example was that a seller contacted me with a fairly high price that I was not able to match. Fortunately, he held on to my postcard and called me back exactly a year to the date after the original call.

He had decided to drop his price by 100K. I could hardly believe it, so I called him back to confirm his price, address, and when he was looking to sell. Sure enough, all it took was some time to pass for his motivation level to increase, and I was able to get a great deal.

Overall, if you are doing marketing and not following up with your leads, that means you have a hole in your net, and you could be missing out on some large catches. Not only should you have a formalized CRM where you follow up with prospects, but you should also follow up with prospects in multiple forms of communication.

This means direct mail, email, phone calls, text, as many forms as communication as possible until you get a yes or no when it comes to selling their property. Fortunately, it is straightforward nowadays to set up a CRM with a follow-up system. For $5 an hour, you can even have a virtual assistant input all your leads and set them up in a follow-up system if you don't have the time.

LAW #44

◆━━━◆━━━◆

Rack The Shotgun

This is a business principle from the legendary marketer Perry Marshall. It's a story about how his friend hitchhiked to Las Vegas when he was 17 and became a pro gambler for several years. He was determined to make it work in this rough-and-tumble city, so he found a mentor, a seasoned gambler who was successful and took him under his wing in exchange for a percent of his winnings.

The very first lesson he taught him was that you need to play games that you can win, or in other words, you need to play people who are not as good at poker as you are (i.e. the marks). His next question was, "Where do I find the marks?" The pro gambler took his young prodigy to a cabaret show with music blaring and everyone drinking.

In his jacket, he always carried a sawed-off shotgun and once they sat down, he pulled it out from under their table. He initiated the gun and ratcheted it back, making a loud snapping noise. He did what's called "racking the shotgun." Just a few people turned around trying to see where that noise came from, while the others were oblivious to the sound and immersed in their nightclub.

The owner came over to their table and asked if everything was okay. The gambler responded, "Everything is great, just teaching the boy a lesson." Then the gambler told the young man, "Did you see those people who turned around? Those guys are not the marks, do not play poker with them." This is an example of racking the shotgun and figuring out whom you need to focus on.

In real estate investing, you could use this principle to only market to those who have already pre-qualified themselves as motivated prospects. Instead of marketing to the entire city, you strategically market to those sellers that are already motivated.

And every city at any given point in the economy has sellers that are significantly more motivated to sell than the general population of sellers. That includes pre-foreclosures, blighted/vacant properties, absentee owners, probate, delinquent taxes, and any other motivated sellers. Only aiming your marketing at the right people makes it more effective.

Overall, most businesses and real estate investors waste a ton of money by not being strategic with their marketing. You need to rack the shotgun as much as you can when it comes to who you market to. Much of the success is in getting the best marketing lists of motivated prospects.

There are numerous sites that can provide these motivated seller lists, such as Alesco Data, Melissa Data, and others. You can also get much of the motivated seller data from your courthouse, and many courthouses have this data online nowadays to make it easier. When it comes to finding deals, make sure you are only aiming your message at the right prospects.

LAW #45

What's In It For Them?

With real estate investing, you should always be talking to other people's self-interest – not your own. You should always ask yourself what is in it for them. This goes for every aspect of the industry, whether you are looking to raise private money, selling a wholesale deal to another investing investor, buying a house from a motivated seller, or even recruiting agents and wholesalers to find you deals. The most interesting conversation you can have with someone is about them and how you can make them more money, do more deals, and grow their own business.

You have to understand, people only care about

themselves. They don't care how much you might make on a real estate deal until you tell them how much they might make or what's in it for them.

For example, when pitching a private lender, let them know they won't have to manage any project, they are investing in a discounted deal, and the loan is secured by the property. Give them the security of the deal as well as how much they could make, and even throw in there how much they could make if they were to invest significantly more.

When talking with real estate agents to help find you deals, you can let them know that if they find you good investment deals, they can be the buyer's agent and the listing agent once the property is listed on the MLS. They can get a two-for-one deal if they bring you deals, which is much more compelling than a standard real estate deal. Now, they have to bring you only good deals, but if you present enough agents with that proposition, they will start sending you leads.

Or if you are talking with a motivated seller, don't brag about how many houses you might buy.

Instead, assure them that you will buy their home quickly, easily, and they won't have to worry about a thing. Always talk about the other person and how working with you will benefit them.

From now on, try to talk about the benefits of working with you. Whether it's a lender, agent, investor, or seller, try to speak to them in a clear and concise way about what they are getting out of the deal. When in doubt, focus on the other person.

In fact, if you want to be considered a great conversationalist, just start asking the other person questions about their life, goals, travel, and anything else they might bring up. People do not care about your accomplishments or anything else until they know what's in it for them.

—————•————————•—————

Take Massive Action

In any endeavor you do, if you want to be successful, you must take massive action. In this section, I will go over specific examples of what I mean. If you're going to become a successful real estate investor, you have to be focused on taking action since most people just dabble. Do not think of yourself as a spectator. You are in the game taking action and making deals happen.

As a real estate investor, the main areas where massive action is needed when getting started are the marketing, networking, and learning aspects of the business. Most new investors start with a marketing campaign and might even get a few leads, but they aren't consistent or don't take enough action to have it stick. For example, if they are doing a direct mail campaign, they will send out 100 letters, get a call or two, but then they will stop marketing and say direct mail does not work.

You need to be disciplined and take enough action to learn the skill set of getting 10 leads per month, 20 leads per month, and on and on until at least 25 leads per month, which is where you start to see results.

That means you might have to send out several thousand letters to motivated sellers – not just a one-time campaign of 100 letters. The same goes for any other marketing campaign you plan on doing, including bandit signs, online marketing, or others. Focus on setting monthly lead goals and building a solid foundation before you try to make a million dollars in house flipping.

While the marketing aspect is the most important, you also need to be taking massive action with networking and learning. When it comes to networking, that means instead of going to one real estate Meetup group like most people, you sign up for all of the real estate-related

Meetup groups, REIAs, and any other cool networking events in your city. This will 3X or 5X your opportunities to meet lenders, partners, wholesalers, and find out about what is going on in your area.

When it comes to taking massive action with learning, this is something every investor needs to focus on. Action will always beat learning, but you need to have a framework from a successful investor about how the business works. You should try to get a mentor in addition to listening to real estate investor podcasts, attending seminars, joining mastermind groups, and anything else that can get you ahead.

Sometimes I might spend two hours or even a full day at a training event, and I've heard 99% of the things before. However, I might learn one or two things that can impact my business and give me an advantage. You should never stop learning, not even once you start doing a deal or two every month. There is always another level.

Taking massive action as a real estate investor, even if it's not perfect, will get you doing deals. For my first couple of deals, I compensated for any lack of knowledge I had with massive action. I was getting so many leads and meeting so many people that I eventually started putting deals together. Start by dedicating at least one or two hours per day to your real estate investing business and then scale it up.

LAW #47

Track Everything

Tracking different parts of your business is an essential part of being a successful real estate investor. You don't need to track everything, but you should track certain things on a monthly basis, like how many leads you get per month, how much marketing you've done, how many offers you've made, and how many deals you got under contract.

Countless studies show that if you want to improve on something, you should measure it. Successful entrepreneur Eben Pagan calls it the "vital stats" dashboard, where you can see the progress and what you have going on in your business. Another name for this is a "Key

Performance Indicator" or KPI.

While you should start out with basic tracking, as you evolve as a real estate investor, you will want to get more advanced with your KPIs. Many of the top investors measure things like profit per deal, marketing costs, average days on the market, the average cost of rehab, and countless other items. That way, if you have 10 or 15 KPIs, you can check on the health of your business at any given time and quickly see where your weaknesses are.

For starting out in this business with tracking, I would get a dry erase board and start measuring on a monthly basis your leads, the networking or educational events you attend, the offers you make, and the deals you get under contract.

You should start with three to five of the most critical parts of your business. If you write these down, I can guarantee you that you will start improving on them, and it will make you a better investor. The metrics I like to track include leads per month, offers made, deals under contract, monthly passive income, and networking events. Most investors don't do this type of tracking so it will give you yet another advantage over your competition.

Stay Lean And Mean

When you are getting started in real estate investing, I recommend staying lean and mean. You need to make a couple of sacrifices to gain that initial leverage to get you to your first couple of deals. You will need money for things like marketing, mentors, and other real estate business costs.

A couple of things I did when I was trying to make it as a real estate investor was getting a cheap apartment, getting a part-time job, as well as making an effort to cut down on unnecessary expenses. Those things alone provided me with an additional $2,000 per month that I could put towards my business.

This helped me pay for my direct mail and internet marketing and gain a solid foundation for this business. I also re-invested the money I was saving into a coaching/mentorship program. By doing all of this, I was fully committed. I almost thought of myself like the *Rocky* movies where he's living in the cheap apartment, waking up early, training, and every now and then, having a cheap beer.

I shake my head sometimes when I hear people say they don't have money for marketing or they don't have time to be focused on investing. They would rather look middle-class and drive an above average car in an above average apartment and watch *CSI Miami* all day than build on their dream. There is no shame in following your dream. Keep in mind that most people don't have the courage to do it.

Once I started doing deals and making good money, I still stayed in my crappy apartment with low expenses. I remember my first breakthrough, where I made close to 80K per month through real estate investing for several months back to back. Instead of upgrading to a luxury apartment, a luxury car, and traveling, I took that money and reinvested it in myself.

I looked up some of the top marketing and business experts in the world and booked three of their events and programs so that I could learn from them. Additionally, I upgraded my camera equipment for my YouTube channel, paid off any last debts I had, and also increased all my credit lines as much as possible while I was flush with cash to give me more leverage to purchase bigger deals. I was growing my power as an investor instead of trying to look cool.

People would ask me why I was going to these weird seminars and spending tens of thousands of dollars on these types of events and programs. Now those same people ask me how I make more in a month than they do in a year.

If you are serious about real estate investing, you should think of ways you can save time or money to get your first couple of deals. Cut down on expenses, get a cheaper place, get a part-time job, and start building your business.

Stay lean and mean. If you are marketing and focused on becoming a real estate investor, you will get there eventually. Then, when you do start making money, be sure to re-invest it in yourself before you begin making lavish purchases.

Zoning

Every real estate investor should have a basic understanding of the zoning laws and codes in your area. It does not mean you have to be a code expert, but if you are active in this business, you will come across different types and styles of properties, and you need to know their highest and best use.

When I was getting started as a real estate investor, I missed out on a multi-six figure profit deal because I did not understand the zoning laws. According to the tax record, the property was zoned so that it could be a five-unit condo building. I did not know this and sold the property as a fix and flip type of deal.

When you start doing marketing and start looking at deals, every now and then, you will come across commercial properties, condo conversion deals, double lots, and much more. If you want to increase your skills as an investor, you should look up what the highest and best use of these different types of properties are.

After understanding my mistake on that deal, I made it my goal to learn everything about zoning in my city, all of which is public information, by the way. I recently bought a commercial property that has many options, including adding a third level, selling it as condos, keeping it as a commercial rental building, or even living there and renting one of the units out.

Try to read as many articles as possible on the different zoning laws, read your city's guide to zoning laws, and talk to as many other investors as possible about the different possibilities.

You would be shocked at how many real estate agents and investors do not have a firm grasp on the zoning laws in your area. Once you become an expert in zoning, you will be able to see deals that other investors don't even know exist, and you will see more opportunities. There are all types of interesting loopholes and possibilities when it comes to the zoning codes, especially if you are in a big city. If you read up on your zoning laws today, you will become a better real estate investor.

LAW #50

───◆────◆───

Embrace Setbacks

When you are getting started as a real estate investor, this is one of the toughest yet most valuable things you can do. Every setback you encounter should make you stronger, savvier, and more experienced. Do not get angry at setbacks.

You should be thankful for them because if you use all of that energy from the disappointment of your setback towards becoming a better investor, then you will see results quickly.

If you learn from five to 10 different setbacks, no matter how big or small, you will become a savvy investor. I will give you a few examples. I missed out on a couple of deals because I did not move fast enough; in fact, I took an entire day to get back to a couple of motivated sellers.

They told me they had gone with a different investor who had met them that day. Instead of getting pissed, I told myself, "Okay, now when I get a motivated seller, I go out and meet them the same day and get it under contract." That minor setback led to some major paychecks after I learned the importance of speed in this business.

Another setback as mentioned earlier was when I missed out on a massive deal because I didn't understand the zoning laws. Instead of sulking and wondering what to do next, I learned the zoning laws better than 99% of the investors out there. I am now working on two commercial deals and probably more in the near future. I used all of that negative energy towards becoming a savvier commercial investor.

A third setback that was common when I was getting started is that a seller would call me and tell me they already had an offer but wanted to see if I could beat it since they had 10 other investors who had sent them marketing. It made me believe that there weren't many deals out there when in reality, I was only getting a few good leads per month.

As a result of getting beat out by these other investors, I focused on learning marketing and building my marketing machine so that I get more leads than I know what to do with every month. And while I still might get those leads where a seller is shopping around, I have 10 other motivated seller leads that I am working on that do not have that same scenario.

I can give you countless other examples of using setbacks to make yourself a better real estate investor. Nowadays, I am grateful for any setback because after 10-20 of these minor or major setbacks – if you learn from them – you become a street-smart real estate investor.

Use every so-called setback to your advantage. They are giving you the chance to improve your ability. Before you know it, you will know exactly what to do in different investing scenarios. I learned this principle from a great book, called *Failing Forward,* which is a must-read for anyone looking to get to the next level.

LAW #51

Focus On Improvement
Over Perfection

Too many real estate investors don't get started
or might spend months and months before they
even look at properties because they think
everything needs to be perfect. What they don't
realize is how un-perfect many successful real
estate investors are. While I always recommend
learning before you take action, you should be
taking action all the time because, ultimately, it is
the best way to learn.

Do not be the investor that goes to seminar after
seminar without trying any of the strategies. Get
out there and start your marketing, your

networking, evaluating deals, and even making offers. I've done marketing and got deals under contract with misspellings on my direct mail postcard before.

I've messed up on tons of deals by not moving fast enough or not running comps accurately enough. In this business, I have found that you will learn very quickly and improve if you just focus on getting better and taking action.

I recommend that you take a lot of action under the watch, so to speak, of a local investor or mentor. That means if you find an amazing deal, but you are not 100% sure, just ask a local investor friend. They can tell you and even assist you on the deal. Better yet, if you are in a coaching program, there are often resources available to help.

Too many new investors spend months coming up with a company name or tweaking their business card a million times. I've heard some new investors ask me what would happen if the other investors at networking groups found out they're a beginner. Who cares?

That stuff is not that important, and a smart investor loves to assist a new investor because they bring them leads and they can possibly partner on deals together. The most important thing is to send your marketing out, network, evaluate deals, and keep improving.

Nothing is ever perfect. There is a famous quote that says, "Done is better than perfect." That is how I see the real estate investing business. Focus on getting better and reaching out to your hard money lender or your real estate investor friend if you have any questions on a deal. I look back on my first years as a real estate investor to my second year, and so on, and it's fascinating how much you evolve yourself and as a business.

Each year, you will do things slightly differently and improve, and your business will be almost unrecognizable from year one to year five, and so on. Taking action is the most exciting part of the business, so get out there today and don't let the false idea of "perfection" stop you from doing deals.

LAW #52

Partnerships

While I believe you should see everyone as a potential partner as one of my aforementioned laws, you simultaneously need to be very wary of partnerships when you are first getting started. I think partnerships can be great, but you have to know how to set them up properly.

When you are first getting started, the likelihood of a deal going south is significantly higher than if you've done flips before. This is especially true if you are partnering with a friend or family member. You should only partner with experienced, successful investors on your first couple of deals and only do it on a deal by deal basis.

When getting started, it is very easy to overestimate the after renovated value of a property or underestimate the cost of repairs. I did this on several properties when getting started. Unfortunately, I had partnered with another inexperienced investor who also didn't know a good deal from a bad one. Somehow, we were able to sort things out, but it could have been worse.

While I think partnerships can be a great strategy, you need to be savvier about it than just partnering with someone because it's your first deal and you're friends with this person. The excitement of starting a new venture and bringing on a friend or family member can often make you pay more for a deal than you should be paying.

I would also not recommend partnering with your contractor. While it sounds great on paper to partner with your contractor, you can just pay a contractor instead of doing an expensive joint venture with them.

Overall, a couple of strategies to ensure your partnership goes smoothly is to only partner with successful investors on your first couple of deals. After making those initial mistakes with partners, I decided from then on if I was going to partner on a deal, it would only be with the top, professional, and experienced investors.

The reason was that I knew they would not screw me over, I knew the likelihood of the deal going through was much higher with them than with a newer investor, and I knew that if they thought it was good, then it must be a good deal since they had done hundreds and hundreds of these deals. Think of it as training wheels for your first couple of deals.

LAW #53

Think Of Business
Like A Game

While you should take your investing seriously, if
you want to be successful, you should also think
of business as a game and play to win. When you
see work as a game, it becomes a lot more fun
and you are going for the top. Since the average
career is only about 30-40 years, you don't have a
lot of time. You might as well go for everything
you can and have fun along the way.

Making money in real estate investing is a lot of
fun, but you know what's even better? Winning
and growing your real estate empire. Reframe the
work you do as becoming a real estate mogul

instead of pushing paperwork if that's what you're currently doing. It will make the business more fun.

Most people don't play to win; they play too conservatively. Dan Kennedy refers to the majority of people as "mental midgets" – not by capacity but by choice. Most people do not think big enough to win because they choose not to. Just by thinking as big as possible and playing that game instead of the game played by the masses, you will leapfrog a lot of your competition.

Every deal I do, every book I read, every person I meet, every seminar I attend – I see it in the big picture of becoming a more powerful real estate mogul. I see it as a game. The most fun thing in the world for me is not even making money but growing and evolving every year. I think you should do the same.

Overall, if you see business as a game, it can make your day to day much more fun, exciting, and fulfilling. There have been countless business moguls, from Mark Cuban to Robert Ringer, and many others, who recommend viewing business as a game to be won.

Your career will be over before you know it so you must go for everything you can in this game. Most people don't go for the top, which leaves a big opportunity for those that are bold enough to play at a high level. If you enjoy the process of evolving as a real estate investor, you will find success.

LAW #54

Be Prepared

The more prepared you are as a real estate investor, the more successful you will be. There are a couple of ways to do that since you never know when you might come across an amazing deal. As long as you are marketing or at least out there looking for deals, there could be one that comes across your desk at any moment, so you must be ready.

There are three main ways that I recommend being prepared so that you can make a deal happen at any time. The first is to have your contracts printed out in your car in a folder or at least readily available. You don't want to have to spend time driving around town and editing an offer at an office supply store during rush hour and barely making your appointment with the seller – ask me how I know.

The second way is to have your financing or cash buyers lined up. If you are rehabbing properties, you should know or have a general idea of how you will finance the property before you go out and start marketing.

That means you should have already talked to some local hard money lenders, as well as private money lenders or other partners. If you are wholesaling the deal, you should have already built your buyer list through networking or by searching for real estate investors on LinkedIn in your area. Or, at the very least, you should know someone with a large buyer list that can send out a deal and partner with you.

Lastly, you should know the comps in different areas around you. During any downtime, you should be reading articles about the real estate values and practicing running comps on actual properties. Many investors I know have an almost encyclopedic knowledge of house prices in the neighborhoods they market to.

You might not need to be that extreme, but you should have a general idea of what a reasonable price is. That way, if you get a super motivated call from a seller, it won't take you very long to run comps since you already know the numbers and you can get out there and make the seller an offer.

Overall, being prepared will make you more comfortable and help you sleep at night. Knowing that you can get a deal under contract at any time is a great feeling and will come across in your negotiations as well. So always make sure you have printed out contracts in a folder ready to go, have your financing or cash buyers lined up, and have a good understanding of the comps in your area.

Work With Integrity

Working with integrity is a key part of being a successful real estate investor. While some investors might be out for a quick buck, the successful investors who have been in this business for a while do not take that same approach.

Having integrity and doing the right thing in real estate investing should be a no-brainer for any investor. However, unfortunately, it is not. One thing I have noticed over the last 10 years or so is that the investors with integrity seem to stick around while the investors that are out to make a quick buck never seem to last very long in the business.

While I would definitely say investors without integrity are in the minority, there are bad apples – just like in any industry. You need to make sure that you operate at the highest level of integrity whenever possible, meaning you don't cut corners, you use licensed and insured contractors when necessary, you don't steal people's deals, you pay your investors back, and in general, you do the right thing.

I remember two investors in particular I worked with that are great examples. One of them ended up going behind my back and stealing a deal from me, which left me furious and out of a profitable deal. I looked this same investor up a year later, and they were out of business and had various legal issues. If you try to cut corners on a deal, you might make money here or there, but eventually, it will come back at you in the form of a lawsuit, dispute, or other issues. Lacking integrity is not a long-term strategy, always remember that.

Another investor I worked with ended up backing out of one of my deals a couple of days before closing. Instead of never hearing from him again, he paid me the earnest money deposit, explained what happened, and was completely open about everything. This second investor operated with a lot of integrity and is still in business and doing very well.

Operate your real estate investing at the highest level of integrity so that you can sleep easy at night, last a long time in this business, and do things the right way. You never want to be known as the investor cutting corners to make a buck. The most successful investors in any market who have been around for a while operate at the highest level of integrity.

The End

Throughout this guide, I've gone over the 55 most unbreakable laws of real estate investing that I have learned over the years. Depending on your market and style of investing, some may be more applicable than others, but ignore them at your own peril. These are all proven laws of real estate investing that have held steady and will continue to be true. If you follow these laws in your own real estate investing endeavors, you will become a better investor – I can assure that.

I wrote this book because I wanted to distill the 55 most important concepts I've learned over the years from being a real estate investor and working with many of the top investors in the country. I am sharing these to help newer investors get to the next level and help grizzled veteran investors refine their skill set. It is now your turn to go out there and apply these principles.

Thanks again for reading this book. I hope you have gained a lot of value from it. I appreciate any and all feedback. If you enjoyed this book, please leave me a helpful review on Amazon so that we can spread the word on the 55 Laws Of Real Estate Investing.

Thanks.

Sincerely,
Jeff Leighton

About The Author

Jeff Leighton is a real estate investor, real estate broker, and bestselling Amazon Author. He has been mentored by some of the top real estate investors in the US and continues to invest in real estate to this day. Over the last several years, he has taught thousands of people around the world on how to get started in real estate investing.

Want More Training?

Go to www.jeff-leighton.com for helpful videos, free resources, downloads, additional mentoring, online programs, and much, much more. You can also text **DEAL to 345345** to stay updated on everything we have going on in the real estate investing world.

Other Books By The Author

Available on Amazon

Follow Jeff Leighton

Instagram.com/J_Late12
YouTube.com/JeffLeighton1
Facebook.com/JeffLeighton5